REALMS
OF THE MOTHERS

The First Decade of Dos Madres Press

DOS MADRES

2016

DOS MADRES PRESS INC.

P.O.Box 294, Loveland, Ohio 45140

www.dosmadres.com   editor@dosmadres.com

Dos Madres is dedicated to the belief that the small press is essential to the vitality of contemporary literature as a carrier of the new voice, as well as the older, sometimes forgotten voices of the past. And in an ever more virtual world, to the creation of fine books pleasing to the eye and hand.

Dos Madres is named in honor of Vera Murphy and Libbie Hughes, the "Dos Madres" whose contributions have made this press possible.

Dos Madres Press, Inc. is an Ohio Not For Profit Corporation and a 501 (c) (3) qualified public charity. Contributions are tax deductible.

Typset in Avenir, Adobe Garamond Pro, Dirkrunner, Ridicule, Zapfino, American Typewrtier, Zoomorphica, Night Sky, Paint Boy, Paulinho Pedra Azul, Platthand Demo, FZ Unique 36, FZ Borders 23, Trajan Pro, & Xenowort

ISBN 978-1-939929-70-9

Library of Congress Control Number: 2016917065

First Edition

DOS MADRES

Executive Editor - Robert J. Murphy
Illustration & Book Design - Elizabeth H. Murphy
www.illusionstudios.net
Realms of the Mothers: The First Decade of Dos Madres Press
Guest Editor - Richard Hague
Project Coordinator - Pauletta Hansel
Intern - Bridget Reilly, Xavier University

Cover Illustration adaped from the original image of "Theogonia Map" by Herwin Wielink. Kind permission to use this image is given by the Pandora Society Role Playing Club.

Dos Madres Press thanks its many wonderful authors for all their support of and faith in the press, as well as permission to include their poems in this anthology.

Many thanks to The Friends of Dos Madres Press for their advice and assistance in furthering the mission of Dos Madres Press.

Realms of the Mothers: The First Decade of Dos Madres Press is made possible with funding from the Ohio Arts Council and ArtsWave and readers like you.

We are looking forward to the next ten years!

REALMS OF THE MOTHERS
INTRODUCTION

In 2004, Dos Madres Press began its first project. This artistic and literary collaboration between Elizabeth Hughes Murphy, artist and designer, and her husband Robert Murphy, poet, was made possible because of the huge advances in small-scale digital printing technology. They were supported and encouraged by both of their mothers, hence the name "Dos Madres" ("Two Mothers" in Spanish) Press.

Elizabeth "Libby" Hart Hughes, Elizabeth's mother, was born in 1923 in western Pennsylvania, graduated from Allegheny College (as did her mother and then her daughter) and Columbia University's Graduate School where she earned her master's degree in education. She was a life-long reader and lover of books. Vera LaVerne Anderson Murphy, Robert's mother, was born in Chicago in 1927, and enrolled in the University of Chicago's Great Books classes, taught at the time by the poet Galway Kinnell, whom she remained in contact with as the years passed. Her curiosity and interest in poetry were spurred on when she heard her son Robert declaiming Dylan Thomas's "Fern Hill" as a high-schooler in what was even then his vatic voice. His passion for poetry (as a young man, he carried volumes of verse to football practice and read from them before games to quell his nervousness) eventually led to the birth of a small literary press. Dos Madres Press, now in its twelfth year, has grown to be an Ohio Not For Profit Corporation and a 501 (c) (3) qualified public charity.

This collection gathers poems from every book published by Dos Madres Press from 2004-2014. Such a large endeavor requires editorial decisions; Pauletta Hansel, anthology administrator, after consultation with Robert and Elizabeth, solicited a few poems of the writer's own choosing, with final selections to be made from those contributions. Each poet would be represented by at least two poems; if a poet had multiple Dos Madres titles, one or two more might be added, while conscious of space considerations. Thus a multiple-title author may have four poems or so; it may also be that he or she only has two or, rarely, one. Final choices were made by myself as organizing editor.

So these poems are taken from the poets' own selections of their best or most representative works. But this still leaves a lot to do for an editor. I might have arranged the poems chronologically, or even merely alphabetically, either by title or author. This seemed arbitrarily easy, even spineless; where's the fun in such pedestrian arrangements? So as I read and re-read the hundreds of possible poems, I tried a few things out. The book's organization was at first unwieldly, clunky. Then it came to me to invent a few categories, or "realms" into which the poems might fall, and that process produced some interesting effects. The categories slipped, blended, overlapped; there came a kind of osmotic cohabitation of the poems in and between their categories, and even a sense that a particular poem could well belong to another realm, some even to a couple of others. This emerging confounding of the categories brought a certain productive tension to the organization, and, I hope, something of the qualities of a poem itself: kinship within difference, relatedness with surprise.

"Apocalyptica" begins the book, rather than ends it. Not arbitrary, it set the obvious pattern for the arrangement of realms, and I followed it throughout. Despite a desire for flexibility and playfulness, sometimes things need to be stiffed into place, else there be monsters.

It is not possible to generalize about all these Dos Madres poets, beyond claiming their universal mastery of craft. Beyond that, the diversity of theme, subject, form, diction, and speaker echoes what I, a former collector of beetles, loved about the insect order Coleoptera: a tremendous range of size, structure, color, habitat, life cycle. Considering that they comprise the single largest Order of Insects, nineteenth-century naturalist J.B.S. Haldane wrote, "The Creator seems to have been inordinately fond of beetles." Likewise, *Realms Of The Mothers* shows in the domain of poetry a rapturous fondness for, and extensive expression of, a similarly multifarious creation.

Richard Hague, September, 2016

vi

TABLE OF CONTENTS

APOCALYPTICA

Ars Poetica

BIOGRAPHICA

BIOLOGICA

COSMOLOGICA

EKPHRASTICA

Erotica

Esoterica

EXOTICA

GEOGRAPHICA

PHILOSOPHICA

PHILOLOGICA

APOCALYPTICA

DAY ONE

The medium-sized city is asleep

The seams in the sky above the medium-sized city have split

Everyone is forgiven and their faces are blown off

Some first got very close to it   An ear to the mulch

Clearly the girl whose jaw, tongue and palate were relentlessly

Necrosed   Clearly

They come charging, these colors

Luminance   Then waves

Helicopters don't even exist

No one is raping anyone now

These colors arrive every ten-thousandth year

Nosegays of fluorescence, spider mums of rain

Someone manumits his slaves

These colors are better than a movie trailer, and faster, and
    thoroughly drenched

From the seams in the sky: a fastness

From the seams: whole and fastened

The concrete is saying it, saying it

1

The blood transfusions took

Our minds are blown   Our plans are fiercely blown

We've sobered up like summer sheets; this galloping is real

Fast and gorgeous they gather

The metastasized colors   And peal into everything

Prepare a poultice, human being

Sweep the remaining rooms

Nathan Swartzendruber
2009 Opaque Projectionist

UNIVERSAL POSTAL

Walking by, I realized the house must
have known its celebrity when it burned—
saw through the second story window to
a carbon-frame of sky and a satellite dish
drooping pointily to the ground and said
to myself, this house was made for pictures.
But every time my feet touched down
on that gray street to take a camera,
a new truck would have parked down front
to carry more of it away—the disappearing house
with cathedral vaults inside, their blackness
the same as height. An orange crab
reaching with a single manic claw pulled
the top window back down into the house,
folded it over. Flat packed it. Wrapped
in cardboard, it was gone.
Instead it left a little hill
where snow would learn to ride down the yard,
a private glacier between the chain link sides.
Where birds might rest or sing, if Spring
is coming back at all.
In the lot's butter dish gutter I found and left
a child's list of flowers with a single entry,
"roses," but space and numbers for a family
of five. Maybe room for them, too.
It's another Saturday of snow, the hot-plate burner
plugged in on the floor where a whistling teapot
could only see the sky. I lay there too

3

dreamily looking through a window with no roof
and weekly snow, sure that José Arcadio Buendia
would stir, faintly in Latin would approve.
Houses too are moving to a warmer clime.

AT A FRIEND'S SUGGTION, LOVECRAFT SAW MARTIN'S MEZZOTINTS

At a friend's suggestion, Lovecraft saw Martin's mezzotints,
an art of the apocalypse, a vast drama of mysterious prophecy,
divine retribution, natural disasters, of Heaven and Hell

and earthly palaces whose sole occupants are the diminutive figures
of Adam and Eve, the angel Raphael, Satan, Sin and Death,
acting out fated dramas in landscapes both monochromatic and bleak.

The immensity of this vision fit the quality of Lovecraft's dreams,
dreams haunted by ancient and enormous beasts,
ancient as stars and blacker than the spaces between them.

Martin's "darkly thunderous, apocalyptically majestic
& cataclysmically unearthly power seemed to hold
the essence of cosmic mystery, a daemon-haunted,

all-engulfing, ravenous gloom of the outer void,
whose *fluctus deumanus* beats perilously
on the frail dykes of this little world of light."

FOREBODING HERALD

Come September, the acorns pelted down
into December. I heard them pinging
helter-skelter on shingles and window pane,
sometimes bullet showers ricocheting,
all through the night as well. The oak senses
something. Will roots rip up? Does it expect
the end? The leaves are green, but woodpeckers
chisel and stab this awful hollow relict.

We live our lives anticipating death
not here and now, but tomorrow—perhaps.
The oak still lives, that huge Goliath,
yet humbly bows to the apocalypse,
as I live for my unparalleled child,
unique seed, but my foreboding herald.

OBLIVION

A ruined temple overlooks the sea,
and time has mingled in the yellow grass
the marble gods and warriors of brass
where lonely weeds enshroud their majesty.
Sometimes, piping an ancient melody
that fills the sky where clouds begin to mass,
a herdsman with his buffaloes will pass,
a shadow in the blue immensity.
Each spring sweet Earth, still hoping to redeem
her ancient gods, on broken columns weaves
worn capitals with fresh acanthus leaves.
But man, indifferent to his fathers' dream,
in midnight's calm without a shudder hears
the Ocean for the Sirens shedding tears.

IDYLLIC LIFE

Idyllic life, what should there be to say?
Idle away the idyll, come what may –
In the sweet spring when roses are in bloom,
Nothing matters, sadness spreads no gloom.

Now in the growing climate of cliché,
Young men blowing, throwing their lives away,
Never knowing wherefore or for whom,
Hurling themselves, like lemmings, to their doom.

Idyllic life, what can we do but play,
And, while we may, make hay and seize the day,
Now that the stored-up honey we consume
Will be depleted in the days to come?

Driven by deprivation and decay,
Whole populations that we kept at bay
Are massing for assault. Their shadows loom
In the redoubts of Kabul and Khartoum.

Idyllic life, when will we have to pay?
Tomorrow or the next day, not today –
In the sweet spring when roses are in bloom,
Nothing matters, sadness spreads no gloom.

L♀SING LITSA

…things which must shortly come to pass….   Rev. 1

From boredom and curiosity, we stopped
at Adrasan, a place our guidebook says
is "post-apocalyptic," found a beach

all weeds and skewed umbrellas, a spit of road,
a row of rusty trailers beyond a shuttered
grocery store. Nothing love would keep,

or only love could keep. Maybe it's just
the women swimming fully clothed, their husbands
in skimpy trunks that pinch their genitals,

but here we say we're happy, say we planned
it so, as we sip our gin at dusk and crack
pistachios, toss the shells to the sand.

Here the body's hold is gone. Each half
awaits its other half while fiercely pulling
to keep its separateness, leaving nothing

either of us now longs for. What's left is prayer:
Lord of this apocalypse, please keep
our love ineffable and dormant. Let the hours

in Adrasan keep stretching endlessly.
Soon enough Fethiyeh, Bandirma
and Istanbul, a taxi to the airport,

then home to love already gone. Here,
unpacked, we're hurtling beyond our bodies.
Our hands will touch, but nothing you'd call substance.

Ars Poetica

C L O C K S

Whatever way I turn, I find a clock.
I see one in that yellow leaf that fell
and in the sharper winds that now propel
the arrow of a migratory flock.
I've watched one where the water eats the rock
lashed by the roaring ocean's rhythmic swell
and heard one in the sigh of a farewell
and in the raucous crowing of a cock.
I feel one now as I count out the beat
of blood my heart is driving to my feet,
which measure out a rhythm with my rhymes;
I hear them ticking like a metronome
where they propel the pendulum that times
this little lyric clock I call a poem.

THE BLIND

It comes to us, as the hunter does
from behind his blind
having waited out
his long day's thinking:

he would have nothing to show
for his hunter's patience.
And tired, only for a moment
closing his eyes,

is suddenly startled to find
himself awake inside,
outside, Orion,
in a star-filled sky, blinking.

VEHICLE

Advancing fragments
into the foreground,
brief and sharp
so that outside-us
will retreat, or flinch
or otherwise admit
what we produce.
It's not much by way
of strategy, or even
worthy of the name
survival, but it gets
what we mean
from here to over
there, dusty, yes,
worn and ragged
at the knees, and yes
camouflaged
by the instant, and yes
transformed entirely
as we'd hoped.

THE MUSE

The chuppah of your words covers my heart
when I decide to wed to poetry,
the language vows I take, some may call art
it's you-my prayer, my muse, that marries me.

I read you in my memory, my mind
where every lovely vowel resonates
so I say "yes" eternal for your kind
this flight of fancy, nothing short of fate.

So strangle me in form, and straddle, too,
and break the glass with screams and shouts of glee,
the celebration's festive when with you,
ketubah seals your poetry in me.

With you, my love, forever I will wed.
You dazzle dreams and saturate my head.

PALIMPSEST: RATUSHINSKAYA

Irina in her gulag cell carved words,
burnt matchsticks on a bar of brown lye soap.
Bone cold, hunger stricken, she wrote, pacing
miles enough to reach Moscow and revise.
Murmuring, Irina incised each line,
each poem (two years, three) on her mind.
Eyes closed, she could see the letters
rise, shadows of inky iridescence.

Once in awhile, guards brought prisoners water.
Before Irina lathered, she traced
her chiseled words, crooning them softly.
Face, arms, thighs, breast scrubbed by graven poems.
Smooth slate in hand, the poet struck a match.
Black fire on strong soap, Irina wrote.

ANDREI ZHDANOV, DIRECTOR OF THE WRITERS' UNION, REPORTS TO PREMIER STALIN ON ANNA AKHMATOVA

She is utterly remote from the People.
She speaks as a unique individual.
Unlike other writers in the capital,
she sings of death, mysticism, doom—

remote from the interests of the People.
Deaf to what is written in her time,
she repeats herself: songs of death,
mysticism and doom

become a blight upon our time
and may corrupt the minds of youth,
the way her verse combines
harlotry with prayer.

Admired by younger minds,
she races frantically between boudoir
and chapel—nun and whore—
she has no concern for the state

only for the boudoir and the chapel.
An overwrought aristocrat
indifferent to the state
and living in the capital

polluting the pages of our journals!
She speaks as a unique individual
unlike other writers.
She is utterly remote from the People.

WHAT I NEED

I need the white space
between the lines,
that sinking-down
between the words;

a good metaphor
to write my life around.
Some days
house will do,

four walls built
brick by solid brick,
undone:
the turning of the seasons

seeping up
from underneath—
crumbling mortar
letting in the spring.

What do I need?
I need a quiet room,
or a noisy one,
my thoughts pushed down

beneath its clamor
and squeezed out onto
whatever page
I find at hand.

No room at all—

a tree stump,
a hard damp piece
of ground.

POETRY AND MYSTICISM, PART TWO

I am sitting with Machado and Lorca
at a table outside Lucky's on St. Charles.
Every twenty-two minutes,
an empty streetcar clatters along the cobblestones.

Lorca says: *There are days*
my shaking tremors will not go away.
Do you know anyone
whose body prays without him?

He tells me to give myself to you,
Poetry, that you would call me
acolyte in spite of my spelling.

Lorca yawns and taps
his iPhone.

Machado chides the final
cadences of day.

You can't be what you were, he says
the tarnish of emerging night
like two crows of easy money,
double nickels on the dime.

Lorca is reading
a text message from God
on his iPhone.

Machado says:
I don't want to hear
these minor threats of evening.
I don't want to hear forged
silhouettes of ragged desire.

Lorca is kissing his iPhone.

Moths fling their tattered bodies
against the window of night.

Machado is kissing Lorca's iPhone.
I am kissing Lorca's iPhone.

Lorca says:
We are the ecstatic émigrés of dream.
Let's abandon our deluded shoes
and ride the streetcar's tail
down the city's dark throat.

ARS POETICA

This is what happens when you become
        committed to poetry:
Your teeth fall out.
        (This happens anyway.)
The heart happens in lunacy.
Weekends and weekdays are indistinguishable
        for the poet.
        (Nights as well.)
We give up hope frequently.
I feel a transplant unspoken.
Then I write.

ALTERNATE READING

Not words on
the page but
pointing into,
perpendicular
homing in

honed edges of
their first letters
glimpsed as
fishtails
schooling off

a Döppler-like
gradation into
unintended else
submersion just
below the page

I call and say
come quick
you'll never guess
but it's too late
Now you have to

The lamp light
on your face
is not the light
I know and now
neither is the face

APOLOGY FROM A
NONFICTION WRITER

It just happens.
I don't intend to lie, not usually.
I start to tell it straight.
Somehow the telling makes things change.

I don't intend to lie, not usually.
Memory lumbers like a bear.
Somehow the telling makes things change.
Old details slip away among the trees.

Memory lumbers like a bear,
imagination buzzing at an ear.
Old details slip away among the trees.
New details find their way on quiet paws.

Imagination buzzing at an ear,
the facts run off to hide in deeper shade.
New details find their way on quiet paws,
settle in, get comfortable.

The facts run off to hide in deeper shade.
I start to tell it straight,
settle in, get comfortable.
It just happens.

KIDS WRITING

i.
At times kids write as if
the person they are becoming
has arrived, using words
they will own
if all goes well
and they suffer the world
to open their voices.

Most times, writing as kids,
they lightning bug emptiness.
Other times they lantern
the dark they stand in.
Each On is bright,
then they Off it.

ii.
When I asked if we could print
a girl's poem about her mom,
their fights, the war, the museum of skulls,
lost brothers, not fighting back, fighting back,
and her mother's single tear,

she answered, "no,"
with a shrug,
and a look that dropped
a gate before whatever sentence
I'd had coming next.

Richard Hague

2004 Burst, Poems Quickly

THE BODY IS A POETRY ANTENNA

To the elbow comes
the pointed remark,
the jibe, the jab
in the ribs
the poem delivers
to the President on the dais.

To the ear approach slowly
all sonics, some
delicate as fawns
in dogwood shade,
some blatant as wide-world
whale blasts
under ocean.

To the glands come
tsunami, hummingbirds,
and no-see- ums,
to the mouth
all the names of God.

To the bowels come
philosophy and charm
and to the brain
come monkey-mind,
insomnia, bright lights,
the soft ballerinas of prayer.

If the body is properly arranged,
or wet with rain,
if it hums like
a newly charged battery,
or is tense and beautiful
as a colt in a field,
it will radiate
sparks:

Left alone in a room,
it will produce
replicas of itself,
and send them out
in a hundred poems,
each with a title
like *Brendan*, or *Sam*, or *Denesha*.

WHY I WRITE

Always the hope
it is more artichoke than onion,
and I am heading toward
a plump, sweet mystery
the surface can never reveal.

Or like tapping mother's crystal goblets,
listening for each resonating tone—
yes this; not that; these together
make a tune. Each note's story
known only in relation to the other.

THE LITTLE TROUT

I wanted to show you
the little trout
that rose up out of the pool
and lay a moment in my palm.
I wanted to show you
her white belly
and the spots of rose
and custard
along her flank.
I wanted you to know
the way she slowly
dissolved
into the bed of the stream.

So here!
In this poem!

A BLESSING FOR
THE FEAST OF ALL POETS

For words, for vowels, for syllables
that purr off my tongue,
I give thanks.
For black ink on a page,
for margins and lines which,
like rules, beg ignoring and for all
punctuation, especially the dash—
forgiving and constant—
I give thanks.
For poets who like miners
go down underground
with only the light
of their own unknowing
to guide them,
I give thanks.
For the ones who do not come up again,
who lay broken beneath
fallen pillar and beams
of the lives that chose them—
though I turn my face
from those cratered lives,
hold their words like a candle
too close to my skin,
then too far from my eyes—
I must still give thanks.
Oh, but those who go down and come up everyday;
who plumb mystery, pull weeds
from the garden, the poem,

the dark path underground;
who sit with me at tables,
hold my words in their hands—
you who are constant as dashes,
as forthright as ink,
I bless you with light
for your journey,
as you have blessed me.

BIOGRAPHICA

FIRST PERSON

My friends are writing
in third person now,
they wander through their pages in disguise,
bone and blood beneath
the paper doll of she.

They are trying
to find the story lines,
delicate crisscross of fate and choice,
plump spider of meaning
at the center of a life.

I am stuck with myself—
the web, the spider,
the sac of eggs,
the wings of flies brittle as last year's leaves—
all me.

OVER DARK ARCHES

Naked and thin and wet as if with rain,
bursting I come out of somewhere, bursting again.
And like a great building that breathes under sunlight
over dark arches, your body is there,

And my milk moves under your tongue—

where currents from earth linger under cool stone
rising to me and my mouth makes a circle
over your silence

You reach through your mouth to find me—

Bursting out of your body that held me for years,
as the rain wets the earth with its bodies—

And my thoughts are milk to feed you

till we turn and are empty,

till we turn and are full.

THE NAP

This afternoon, luxury,
I lay down in the shape of my body.
In these clothes that no shape matters,
I may have dreamed.
But, here, brought back in time,
turned out of sleep, the sun
hung in the balance of its journey:
        four o'clock
on the down-ward way to five.
Could have been of a different light,
        but wasn't.
That those birds in the pig-nut tree
outside the bedroom window spoke
without caring, in what language
I may have overheard,
was, perhaps, in retrospect,
an over hearing. The wind
did its windy thing. I cannot
explain how in the leaves there are
semaphores of meaning,
and I in no hurry to understand.
Or why the telling of this moment
is my own to tell.
Nothing happened. Nothing
I can say of importance.
Maybe a few walnuts fell
onto the drive.
I later found some there,

last year the same,
along the graveled curve.
Where, once, I sat in a dark time
brooding, weighted
with the freightings of the world.
And was of matter's ruin.
But out of ruin strayed,
new-born and still
shaky on the palings of its day.
Stood, up from the shadows,
  a fawn,
light on dappled fur.
And finding *me* of little interest
   walked away.

NUMBERS AND ROOMS

I began as something shameful, something flawed,
when I faced the stark reflection of myself
in the gold bathroom mirror, kept my mouth closed

in fear, saw my father's jaw drop open
when he'd spring my door, inside a lover
piled on me, the window screened by oleander.

I rode asphalt crests through hills that summer,
stink of skunk-spray, aloe, honeysuckle, cows.
I parked—lights flicked through smog—eased down my zipper.

I rode all night in a white Camaro
with a young Filipino who picked me up
in the Brass Rail. He pushed my head to his lap

and made me love it, made me see my body
furtively, growing, shrinking from itself.
When he rolled the white door open, I rolled free.

Seeking what? Sidling into nights unseen,
cruising men with molded torsos guiding their hips
through huge underground discos, one-night scenes,

a fraud to myself. Where else if not here
could eyes dart black pools of mirrors, numbers and rooms
where another pair of eyes waited for me?

The stiff plunge in beneath a whirring fan.
Afterwards, the twin robes printed with cranes.
Too scared of what I was, what I might be,

the naked fear of discovery,
(which, in my flight home, pitted me against sunrise
and the dignity of tenderness)

to feel what a man might feel for a man
in the flash of seed sprung from willing triggers
duelled beneath our faces dumb with pleasure.

WRITTEN ON THE BACKS OF SPEEDWAY GAS RECEIPTS

Kilometers are shorter than miles.
Save gas, take your next trip
in kilometers. – George Carlin

Tran# 237612
December 20, 2008

Just as I begin
to pump my gas
I look down
and realize
I am wearing
only a slip.
One by one—
in a show of solidarity—
other pumpers strip
to their underwear.
Only the illegals
hesitate.

Tran# 564441
January 12, 2009

The man
in the last pump bay
begins to sing
Greensleeves
so loud and longingly
that we each file by
and drop coins
into his commuter cup.

Tran# 784115
March 18, 2009

Today, the station
is busy. There are
2 trapeze artists,
1 lion tamer, 4
clowns piling
out of an old
Alfa Romeo Spider,
1 disheveled ringmaster
and 4 snow removal
guys. The snow guys
are buying hot dogs
with mustard and onions.
There are 2 small children
sitting alone in a car
eating cotton candy
for breakfast.

Tran# 256114
April 4, 2009

2 dogs in the car,
3 bays down
are holding
a lady hostage
while her husband
pumps gas. They're
roughing her up good.
They want money. I think
her husband is mouthing
help us to me, but
I decide
to stay out of it.

Tran# 421587
June 1, 2009

The man at pump 2
is wearing a living room.
Soft gray walls, a blue
checked couch. A green,
gold and rust colored
throw pillow
down the front. No
bric-a-brac.
He's obviously used
an interior designer. He
looks like he wants to
invite me over.

PEDDLER

This is a sample of my goods.
My pans are useful when all others fail.
You can leave it on the stove, and it will not blacken.
Bang it against a rock; it will not dent.
It is more reliable than some husbands.
I see by the nod of your head you agree.

Here is some white linen.
Notice how it can wipe away sadness.
You can wave it as the solitary men pass by.
I can tell by your blush this would be welcomed.

This is something special. Only for you.
It is a sponge from an ocean of laughter.
Soap your breasts. When you are dry,
you will find your husband's fingerprints.
I know that this is what you desire most.

THE KNIFE SHARPENER

I sharpen knives for a living.
Everyone knows when to expect me.
The women line up with their dull knives.
They wait their turns like waiting for a kiss.
They act embarrassed while waiting.
They watch the grinder send sparks into their air.
They watch as the knives become useful again
and not at all like a lazy man in the gutter.
They see the edge become sharp as a rumor.
They could split a hair by dropping it on an edge.
They are almost hypnotized watching the stone spin.
During this time they could be thinking of moonlight.
For all I know they could be watching to learn something.
They could be thinking of shaving a husband
or cutting off the head of a chicken, and how it is the same.

I just sharpen knives like they sharpen their tongues.
I cut across conversations.
When they see me, they are no longer hanging laundry,
or tanning their bare legs, or kneeling in a pew.
When they hear my wheel grinding its teeth,
they stop whatever they are doing,
even if they are doing nothing.
They could have dropped a basket of freshly picked eggs.

I only come once a month.
If I come too often, they discover they do not need me.
If I do not come for more than a month, then it is a drought.
They have found someone else capable of the same task.
It is the same as replacing a cow that no longer gives milk.
They replace me like a lover who has no sense of leaving.
They replace me like tossing out dirty water.

I may be only a knife sharpener, but I bring them what they need.

And when I am done, I pack up and go to the next village
where already the knifes are as dull as life.

IT WAS THE 70s

      and the carpets
were wall-to-wall. My mother
     had a plastic rake
she used daily to keep the nap
of her green shag piled high.

     After raking
the sin was to move around
     and mash her plush.
*For Christ's sake, Jimmy, can't you
stay put in one place?*

     I just raked.
It was easier to head outside,
     even on a January
afternoon already dark, snow
up to my knees,

     and nothing
right or wrong to do. My dad
     home early
for once found me lobbing
snowballs up

     onto the roof.
*Whatcha doin'? Mom just raked
     the rug.* He nodded,
plucked a lump of snow,
squeezed, and flung

           a perfect strike
at the bird feeder planted
           twenty paces deep
into the yard. Put a nice crack
in the nearside

           plate glass,
then packed another tight one
           that smelled faintly
of Luckies and handed it to me.
Have at it, kid. I'll cover you inside.

SELF PORTRAIT HOLDING
THE CAMERA AT ARM'S LENGTH

These love-hungry hours of the new century
wait like something silent and bleeding on the kitchen table.
We sip wine from jelly jars and listen to the smack of the night
beetle on the kitchen window.
I eat the I Ching and you, my lover, sing
songs my mother never taught me.

I wrote the forty-one verses of the universe on an acorn.
I have the manifest humility of the peacock.
I am the cat that trods to all the measures of the music,
the russian blue who left the mouse's head
at the foot of your mother's bedstead.
I the thieving squirrel of beech tree birdseed.
I the purple rook who steals
only the best handmade shoes.
I am the fallen timber of forlorn doves, the smitten fly,
the undone virgin's slipper, the half eaten book.
I am the ugly stepson of tomorrow, bastard
lice of Frank Stanford,
mud brother of every dead Marine.

As a boy I rode school buses down washboard gravel roads,
copping a nod and popping a rod every morning.
I kissed a sliver sandwich and thought of sex
every seven seconds.
You say I was a tender leaf of April
bruised by God's thumbnail,

seduced by salvation
and an eighth grade student-teacher,
Ms. Tongue-of-Fire, she whose kiss could lick
thirteen coats of paint
from the bulkhead of a battleship.
I the moaning capillaries of Montagues and Capulets.
I waged war on tent worms and tree frogs and saw the last
drop and final word of rain.
François Villon would not claim me, he wouldn't
pay a measly fifteen bucks a month
for child support. When I was a boy,
my only friends were Beetle Bailey,
Barney Beagle, and Beowulf.

When you speak of life and love, remember
the ruined chimneys, brick pillars
choked with snakebit kudzu. Remember
the tumbled mansions of the coast,
the shotgun shacks gone to sea,
Katrina portraits weather-worn and wormwood.

My dear, you lie awake at night
and think of life and love and hear
my dream ponies kick and crib
their pole-barn stalls. You see smoke
dribble from the nostrils of marble statues.
You know their cold eyes
follow the slightest dust mote
lighting on the sheets
and your soft wrist.

You know me.

BROOKLYN NAVY YARD

My mother gives her

Name: Florence Gluck
Age: 18 (false).
Trade: stenography (true)
Hair: dark   Eyes: brown
Height: 5' 5 ½" Weight: 116
Moles on neck and arm

Florence Gluck, Yeoman 3rd class,
U.S. Naval Reserve Female.

Florence, delighted, writes,
"How do you like my uniform?"

She poses proud, white skirt to her ankles,
white jacket one stripe on the sleeve,
floppy bow tie, straw hat.   In winter,
she'll change to blues and a flowing cape.

The cost of her uniform —
    each skirt and jacket $7.50,
    hats $4.50, cape $25 —
deducted from monthly pay.

She's issued a *Bluejackets Manual*,
rules "every man on board ship must know,"
(discipline, battle, shipboard duties)
writes her name, green ink, on the flyleaf.

She is one of 12,000 female yeomen
taking dictation, typing, filing,
translating, phoning, analyzing
the huge paperwork of war
so Navy men could fight
on ships to make the world secure.

Service done, Florence is rated
Proficiency in Rank: Good
Sobriety, Obedience: Excellent
and given medals to commemorate
the Great War to End All Wars.

Ruth D. Handel
2013 Tugboat Warrior

MEDALS AWARDED MY MOTHER

Imagine you weighing them
in your hand, your fingers
stroking the embossed

rifle-ready soldier, stern victory angel,
counting the roster of nations.

The Great War for Civilization.

The War to End War.

Did you ever weep
for that naïveté and cynicism, Mother?

Ribbons, one blue and white, the other
rainbow, both faded.
Fasteners rusted.

Who pinned on your medals?
An officer, praising your service
or some local politician

or did they leave it to you
to fasten them on
in front of a mirror at home?

I tried to put
one of your medals on.
The pin wouldn't bite into fabric.

Did you look at your medals often,
show them to lovers,
or remember them

only when you came across
the small white box at the back
of a bureau drawer?

My life moving still,
older than you ever were,
fumbles over artifacts.

COUNTING COUPONS WITH THE ITALIAN LADIES

My mother marched across the street, convinced
Al Vicks to give me a job,
anything at all would be fine,
as long as it kept me off the beach,
as long as my 15-year-old body
in the pink bikini wasn't beckoning
to every boy who passed by.

The next Monday, there I was
the youngest girl at PA Food Merchants Assn.
eight to five
third floor
screeching window fans
counting coupons with six loud ladies
sliding those coupons into wooden slots
Palmolive on the far left
Colgate in the middle
Campbells on the right
ranking them
5
10
15
cents.

There I was
the only worker under 50,
the only one who didn't speak Italian.
The ladies bellowed *scusa, aiutare, cuore, luce.*
Sometimes they fed me bites
of their lunches, leftover casseroles,
garlic, flat noodles.

Angie, Lena, Marion, Maria
and two others whose names are gone now.
They talked about grandchildren, bunions,
red peppers on sale at the A&P,
stroked my hair, called me *bella,*
things my mother never did.

CLAIMS OF HOME

How much were you like us? How could we know?
When Ulysses floated into my shop, careworn,
Smudged like a burnt tin can just plunked ashore,
His hood fell away, and I could see his face.
So changed. His eye seemed fixed on final scenes
From so much gazing forward into sealight.
Distraught, he scanned my shelves, peering behind
The floured bread and raisins for his past.
There was nothing back there for him to buy
That could redeem the days when these raw boards
Were native to his smaller feet, when my sweets
Smelled so alluring. The sea was over,
The hard world gone, and there could only be
The end of things: the slow walk home to claims
Of home, uncomprehending glances, Penelope.
But I, who played so little part in them,
Recalled beginnings: How alert the lad
Grew when he saw a cake worth stealing, then
Refrained, canny of consequences, wise
To outcomes even then. A moment passed,
And he was on the shore, a man rigging
Masts and overseeing oars, a chosen one,
One of the larger roughs sailing for Troy.
Yet like the rest, he once had been a boy.

FROM THE VIEWING STAND

Woodmere Club, 1938

I am four. Nobody told me
how to climb this marquee.*
Scary heights, all those
empty benches. Sky   far
out there and the trees,
I'm almost as high as
those leafy branches.
Mommy and Daddy are far
down, they warned me
I must stay up here.
I don't want to stay
or go. I only know
how far it is between us
and how hard he swings.
Sometimes he misses but
he keeps on
swinging. Oh. And I know
she's very careful, her little
white skirt is careful, her arm
is too, slowly going back and
out and hitting, she hits
very carefully, she watches that
little ball, she doesn't look anywhere
else, not up here, not at Daddy,
(and whatever she's smiling at
in the air, I never saw her so

happy except in the mirror
when she's getting dressed
and I'm hiding behind her bed
to watch her put on the blue gown
and those tiny pearls.)

Only once, I think, she looked at
Mr. Cozzoloo, when he moved
to the white line near her (I tried
to hear what he said, I think he said
nice.) She only looks at the net
while she goes around to the other
side after a long time. That's when
they shout set, and Daddy gets even
more serious. He rushes to the back of
his court and stands there hunched over
his racquet, bending his knees up and down,
one knee, then the other one, over and over
like marching but not moving. He's ready.
Then, before it all starts up again with
the ball, she turns her head and squints
and looks up at the marquee and waves,
as if I'm a grown-up on a train
and she's doing the fare-well part of
a story again. But Daddy frowns,
he hits his racquet on the ground.
He wants her to pay attention. Is that
her job? Mr. Cozzoloo has a big wrist-
watch he watches. Why am I the one
going away? It's summer. Soon I'll be
old enough to go in "the deep" of the sound
where the dock has dangerous barnacles

and it's so dark way down nobody can
touch bottom. But I'll be brave,
I'll be out of the "crib" by the sandbox
where the little kids kick and pretend
they're swimming. I won't wear a life-
preserver or a cap either, and I'll float
whenever I get tired of moving
my arms and legs. I'll know how good it feels
to be all alone in the sun in the deep cold.

Mommy says I can go away to day-camp soon,
and then, when I'm ten, to sleep-away camp.
They say they're teaching me things, they even
ask if I want to come down closer, sometime,
and have a proper tennis lesson. I say yes,
but I know the secret of being in this
family already— in our house, and at this club.
Look how good I am at climbing
the highest white railings all by myself.

*"Marquee" was the word used for the viewing stand.

Mary Margaret Alvarado
2013 Hey Folly

IT STARTLES

Who can punctuate it? Wife.
The unplantable blacktops in the past
of my wife. The hurricaned
petals. The combustible joints
of wife. My wife getting naked
under stars in a car.
The chiseled and serif
typeface of wife. The radiance:
her fancies and goodnights.
Natural law's deduced from such
movements. In the house whose root
is my life. Dusky,
sometimes a lioness
sleeping. Taking dictation
for briefs. Courting in malls
gone to seed. What astonishes.
Who? Cur'rants, coop'ers, wife.
For'bear'ance, for.bear.ance, life.
We refused the agents
of mansionization, my wife.
We put the palm chakras
over the eyes, which eat light.
Yet we never rolled a rug
and played a gramophone.
And we never bit the sugar
knuckle to the sugar bone.

Wife, you say you saw
the hook and carcass
swing in the door.
Tell how we took a bus to the beach
to watch the cook fires go. The waves
were mushy, the dark
fettered down. Are pictographs
better? Is archness the answer?
Bonny. Ennui. To do it
without the assistance of machines.
Among pleas. For a time, wife and I,
we were festively clothed. The flung,
stony planets made wishes on us.
Blinking wife, thinking wife, my piebald
stitched, my soldered life.
Now! The cold! Is! Past!

Henry Weinfield
2005 The Tears of the Muses

AUGUST:
THE LAKE AT NOTRE DAME

"ne l'aere dolce che dal sol s'allegra"
Dante, Inferno 7.122
"in the sweet air that's gladdened by the sun"
Allen Mandelbaum, trans.

Mid-to-late summer on a sunny day:
The air is clear; there's no humidity.
A bright-blue sky, expansive and serene,
Bends over tree-tops, blending with their green.

Swans with their cygnets, soon to be full grown
And, in their turn, rear cygnets of their own,
Circle the surface, mirrored in the wake
Of sunlight glimmering on the glassy lake.

Who could be sullen in the afternoon
– In the sweet air that's gladdened by the sun,
Or fail in gratitude when song-birds sing,
A Great Blue Heron suddenly takes wing?

Our lady stands upon her golden dome
– In this place, which in some sense is our home,
With outstretched arm and blessings to confer
Even on those who don't believe in her;

And from the depths of her untroubled eye
Her gaze goes out into the bright-blue sky,
Where in the distance wisps of cloud are swirled –
As if there were no troubles in the world.

to Nicholas Ayo, C.S.C.,
on the occasion of his retirement

MARY DESCRIBES THE
ANGEL TO ELIZABETH

Imagine the look of a man
who will never be a husband:
he had a special thinness,
a resistance to being fed.
He roused in me such freedom!

And when he moved, it was
with the fresh angularity
of adolescence, even though
he was old, old, his skin
sheer as glass, fragile.

He roused in me such fire!
And oh, yes, I was willing.
I told him, "I will." I did not
mean, "I will do this thing."
I meant, "I will it. I will it."

WHAT THEY CALL ME

Ark of the Covenant, Cause of Our Joy,
Dispenser of Grace, Eastern Gate,

Flower of Carmel, Health of the Sick,
House of Gold, Immaculate Mother,

Lady of Sorrows, Mirror of Justice,
Morning Star, Mystical Rose

Queen of Peace, Refuge of Sinners,
Rose Ever Blooming, Seat of Wisdom,

Star of the Sea, Tower of Ivory,
Woman Clothed With the Sun.

I am all of that and more.
I am none of that and less.

I am as you are: a woman who
lived and loved and suffered.

OPEN WINDOW

The woman who chose to do without her other breast
does not fear cancer recurring so much
as she's grown tired of references to Amazons,
their bowstrings whirring unimpeded, arrows flying undeflected to their mark,
tired of being cajoled into courage.
    Besides, her one breast felt lonely lopsided silly.
She prefers how the surgeons froze her nipples and reattached them
on the smooth slight mounds of scar.

She remembers her younger body,
the glee when her mother finally said ok
she could sleep at the foot of the bed, her head
under the open window, wear only the bottoms
of seersucker 'jams. That's how she knew summer
was really here.
                She can just hear the refrain
" . . . *on Blueberry Hill,*"
                    the screen door bang
as Helen leaves for the day,
and the bedtime sky isn't all the way dark.
She can make out the swing set, clothes line, their garden—
rounded shapes of darkness she knows are tomatoes, kale, beets.

She wants to sleep that way tonight,
promising dreams, a light breeze playing
over her almost androgynous chest.
She wants her younger sister in the twin bed, their older sister
down the hall, grown-up voices drifting through the deepening night,
the dog sighing as she settles under the window. Sugar
we named the caramel-colored stray, "Sugar, here girl."

GRANDCHILDREN

They disappear with friends
near age 11. We lose them
to baseball and tennis, garage
bands, slumber parties, stages
where they rehearse for the future,
ripen in a tangle of love knots.
With our artificial knees and hips
we move into the back seats
of their lives, obscure as dust
behind our wrinkles, and sigh
as we add the loss of them
to our growing list of the missing.

Sometimes they come back,
carting memories of sugar cookies
and sandy beaches, memories of how
we sided with them in their wars
with parents, sided with them
even as they slid out of our laps
into the arms of others.

Sometimes they come back
and hold onto our hands
as if they were the thin strings
of helium balloons
about to drift off.

GODS AND MONSTERS

Like a sack of letters I come back to you,
My face as thin as love on onionskin,
My serifs fading, the memories back
To their old tricks again, back to renew
Some glimmer in the mind. But as you spin
And dive in your bubble bath, rise to wash walls
Assiduously, covered with suds, you are a true,
If small, Neptune imbued from head to fin
With all the salty life my long days lack,
Plunging with your trident through the squalls.

Beyond your mythy brink, your brother draws
Funny mechanical monsters. Twirling
A strand of hair, on his belly, he gazes
At the meshing gears, the fierce, archaic jaws,
And pauses. He sees a sadness swirling
Amid any villain's motives. Hounded,
His new Godzilla, fearing the vengeful laws
Of cruel little men, begins hurling
Down Tokyo. Thus, while the Ginza blazes,
The beast himself is the one who's wounded.

Evening deepens; I stumble from your room,
Past the millions of tiny cars, with a sense
Of dazed elation. Some sweetness lingers:
Prismatic color off the bubble, some
Dawnlight of sympathy and ambivalence
Where you were. Then, like jagged streaks of light

That break off after a dive, as the diver comes
Coolly upon a darkness utterly dense,
Consolations disperse. Through my fingers
The gods and monsters rise into the night.

I PLANT YOUR CROSS

for T.

1.

November in Oaxaca, I honor you
with chocolate skeletons, pine incense, mescal.
The borrowed grave is marble, vine-festooned,
a young girl, family estranged on All Soul's Day.

I offer calla lilies, chalice-shaped,
to right the fallen urn. Let's trickle spirits
in her mouth and clink a toast, *To stubborn.*
You left no hallowed ground, but I have come.

2.

At Houston's Rothko Chapel, I fix upon
a canvas of your shadow, graceful gull
who skims the sky, her wings full-open—
a periwinkle dawn. I stand and follow,

who knows how long? Who knows when the bird
begins to scream, to fly, to hide herself
inside another frame against the wall? Here,
sulfuric mist, a burst of marigold.

3.

In a cabaña by the sea, it all comes clear:
*It's no one's fault when sirens call an end
to madness.* So say the tide's night breath,
the moon's marred face, the palm that drops

74

sweet fruit on shrugging beach. Still, I must write you twelve,
and some years later, twirling barefoot, alone
before the mirror, headphones on. Walking
blue horizon, I almost hear that song.

THE JELLYLIP SMOOCHERS

At six my Joan of Arc commands a troop
of first-grade girls. When she declares war
they follow her into battle with the blind
obedience of baby ducks. Racing across the
playground in search of the enemy, they spy
one, a little boy leaning against the water
fountain tying his shoelace. Like killer bees
they swarm, stinging him to the ground with
kisses, then swell up fat as cats after a canary
lunch while he deflates into last week's party
balloon. Afraid his friends will see him crying
the child remains face down until my daughter
guides her warriors on a new quest. Word
of Joan and her band of lip-glossed warriors
spreads among the school kids like the flu.
The boys dub them "The Jelly Lip Smoochers."

Now that first-grader, grown into a take-charge
woman, brushes her husband away like a pesky
fly, insisting she is busy and he is not to bother her
with kisses. The rules of engagement have changed.
The war continues.

BOUGHBROKE

"Don't sing *bough broke*, Grandma,
don't sing *bough broke*." –Max, 3, 1995

Because I loved him too much
and having all those kids was
what I thought I did for him. So
when he socked me in the jaw
or kicked me out of bed it led

not to less love but rotten hopes,
old clothes and hidden thoughts
wrapped and tied with furious knots.
I didn't stop— what? —thinking? No.
Tears? He hated those. The shouts?
His got louder. Hiding? He could
find me everywhere. Oh God, I didn't stop
shielding my eyes, covering up. I kept on
being the one

I couldn't stop. It led to more. Yards
of the high trapeze. More
of *Henry IV* and comic relief,
those ridiculous babies climbing on
my hips. He assigned them
five heavy names that held
around my wrists, so the cold
shame was blurred in nursery buzz,

so when at last the snow
came in the door and all the evergreens
we'd planted filled the space to breathe in,
so to breathe was hard and the walls
leaned in and the windows stuck,
I cracked . . .   the glass.
If he kicked me one more time,
I swore, I'd call the cops. He did
and I did and got out through
a tiny window in the dormer over the pool
behind the chain link fence,

alive. I still had energy
to fly and the sense to drive.
I laughed, and sang the nightmares out
swearing never again

to cringe or stoop or pull my hair back
in a plain chignon. I swore to fight,
I swore to keep my kids,
I swore the house was mine, I locked
the deed in a vault, I lost weight and
did not wipe the "red paint" off
my lips. I rode. I flew.

I didn't swear off men. I found myself
innumerable beds, I raised my flag
where estrogen grew in terra cotta pots
and my gypsy hair was a cloud
around my head. I was the opposite of
dead. I gathered topaz rings, black onyx,
cowries, coral from deep reefs
as gifts. I traveled wide and hard and

circled back. Under all the spilled seed
was too much something
to carry off. It was late at night, I slept
well, I slept like my babies in the tree
until the red wind blew
and the bough broke.

THIS IS NOT A POEM IT'S A LETTER TO A DAUGHTER OR NOTES FOR A MEMOIR

—for Miranda

The days have been bright and breezy
and cool in the late-afternoon shade.
The birds have been rapturous
and varied at your mother's feeders.

Among the visitors, raucous sparrows,
unruly and unkempt, are my least favorite.
We hear them gather before they
pounce on the feeders, winging straight
over the lattice fence and into the redbud
or the golden rain-tree.

They gang up on sunflower seeds,
those little bullies of the bird playground.
Thankfully, your mother feeds
other, more alluring birds.

The mourning doves congregate in their head-
bobbing pairs, woo-woo-wooing as they land,
one, two, beneath a feeder.
They're content with drop-dross,
the countless husks and seeds that
fall on the grassy hill.

Rose breasted grosbeaks arrived last week
and seem to be gone already—like listening
to a White Stripes song too young.

The cardinals make a racket, too,
but tastefully and from a distance.

(I told your mom
the cardinals of my boyhood
sang, Murray, Murray,
Murray-Murray-Murray
in the hardwood forest
around the house. She said:
They don't seem to say that now.)

The blue jays are the serious
bullies, really, of the feeders,
especially the tray feeder
hanging in the dogwood out front.
They arrive like pterodactyls,
scattering the Carolina chickadees,
the house finches, and the wren.

Only the hummingbirds, sipping your mom's
sugar-water, ignore the squawking jays—
the hummingbirds and that cantankerous woodpecker,
who bitches at me from Mr. John's ancient live oak
every time I walk into the front yard.

I dropped a few limbs today
from the elm behind the house
and the hackberry along the driveway.
One branch fell and nearly crushed the young

sunflowers growing beneath the tall
feeder in the dogwood. I threw the limbs
over the fence on the hill behind the house,

and not long after—
while I raked leaves
from where we cut the old magnolia—

I heard seven pistol shots beyond the fence,
9-millimeter. Probably kids
blasting into the berm above the house,
where the ash and water oak shade
that piece of Main Street blocked off
ten or more years ago.

I was thinking about the time some kid
tried to shoot Blue but missed the dog.
The round punched through the high window
and lodged in the wall above the living-room couch.
We had just returned
after picking you up from school.
You left your book bag on the couch
before going to your room.

I know you remember.
You were in tenth grade,
I think, at Warren Central, right?

Anyway, I thought about all that today,
but only briefly and without rancor.
How could I feel rancorous today,
when I saw the neighborhood
swainson's hawk dipping first one,

and then the other outstretched wing
on a wind I couldn't feel but only see
swaying the pine-tops?

She was hunting up there,
looking down with those eyes.

Three mornings ago, as I backed down the driveway,
she swooped over the side lattice fence
and over the hood and windshield of my car,
and I thought: Those little birds better watch out.

This morning, I saw her take a baby bluebird
from the grass beneath a red oak.
She flew over me, and if I reached out my hand
I could've touched that young thing
screaming for its parents
who chased the hawk.

This afternoon,
I found eight mockingbird feathers
beside the Japanese maple
your mother and I planted two days ago.

How can I help but love
such a hungry bird?

Anne Whitehouse
2012 The Refrain

MOTHER AND CHILD

A gray mid-March day:
the bare branches lean
across the blank sky.
All colors moved indoors

where my daughter and I
play with her toys
laid out on the rug:
rattles, dolls, and trucks,

nesting plastic bowls,
a flock of yellow ducks.
Shakily she stands,
her tongue darting like a snake's

between her pink gums,
she smiles, claps her hands,
and bangs the shell table
made by Great-grandpa

of rare wormy chestnut.
Its submarine treasures
are sealed under glass.
Her palms leave sticky smears.

She reaches for my face,
her hands stroke my ears
and clasp round my neck,
her cheek against my skin.

I breathe her mild scent,
I take it all in.
My baby pulls me hard,
she is so insistent.

She turns to press
her forehead against mine,
and the world seems to shrink
as if it held just us,

a game that lovers play.
Did babies play it first?
Now in my arms she lies,
her mouth at my breast,

a soft, avid pump.
She clutches me, and then
relaxes into sleep.
Night falls. The minutes spin

away in the dark.
Now I'm forgetting this;
I must have dozed off, too.
She sucks in dreamy bliss,

as her sweat gilds my arm:
matted hair, cradled head.
Love flows in me like a
river in a muddy bed

that roars around stones
shedding mist and spray,
and swells to meet the sea,
forever carried away.

Ephemeral baby
whose growth will replace you,
shadow and memory
till time will erase you,

To show you as you were,
my quicksilver daughter,
I fix you on this page:
Claire, eight months of age.

TAKING DINNER TO MY MOTHER

My mother sits on the edge of her bed,
a scarf on her head to hide the gray hair
she can no longer manage to dye black,
her flesh falling away from the frame of
her face and shoulders, loosened by the loss
of weight when the body betrays the soul,
when the body's pain forbids all desire.
But tonight she is hungry, and I have

come bearing corned beef and pastrami, bread,
sour pickles and a kasha knish.
I help her to the table in slow, small

steps, a *pas de deux* we have carried on,
I realize, for almost sixty years, and
I think of how, some time before, I held
my daughter's hands, bent over, as she learned
how to walk – the fact of balance, which we
live with until it abandons us – and
how my mother, in a photograph, held
me in the same way. Earlier today,

I had stopped at a café and, sitting
still for a moment, looking up from a
book, I watched how, at a nearby table,

a new mother fed her infant daughter,
who sat up in her baby carriage, some
bits of crustless bread held between thumb and
forefinger, while her grandfather talked on,
the smell of her mother's hand mingled with
this first food, a small bird in her nest. At
my mother's table I fix her sandwich
and tell her about her granddaughter who

met a boy for a moment in a flea
market, who is now a first love, but my
mother's eyelids are starting to lower,
her head nodding forward slightly, so I
gather her up and walk her back to her
bed, sit her down and swing her swollen legs
up and then under the covers, turn off
all the lights but one, close and lock the door.

READING ALOUD TO THE
CORPSES OF MY PARENTS

The speed of light slows to a crawl—.
It falters—. Then it grabs a hold
of wheelchair chrome, of wedding gold—.
They're barely burnished. That is all
the light I have to read by.

Half filled glasses in their hands
are tipping—almost spilling. Lapse
and loss have given birth to gaps
I need to fill. My voice expands
the silence it is freed by.

"Your father wants to hear you read—
from your own book." So I brewed tea.
And gladly silenced the tv.
Their eyes closed almost instantly
the moment I'd begun.

Yet if I stop, they soon protest,
they're wide awake with loving smiles—
a Pharaoh and his Queen beguiled
by prospects of eternal rest:
"Just read us chapter one."

It can't be true my book's that boring.
Her dropped jaw. His tilted head.
They cannot possibly be dead,
I tell myself, I hear them snoring.
Such peace, I can't deny them.

The force of breath descends to drift—.
It fades—. Then steadies to a wheeze.
And in that all but failing breeze
two sails too briefly sigh, and lift
a voice to lullaby them.

(Massapequa, Long Island—2008)

90

Anne Whitehouse
2012 The Refrain

THE DECISIVE MOMENT

The decisive moment, it is the simultaneous recognition, in a fraction of a second, of the significance of an event as well as the precise organization of forms, which gives that event its proper expression.
Henri Cartier-Bresson

On a glorious June evening
after the retrospective exhibit
of Cartier-Bresson's world-spanning art,
I strolled into Central Park,
and left the path to climb the rock.

Below me, a woman approached the arch under a bridge
trailing two leashes connected to twin beagles.
The heightened perspective, the swirls of motion
made a picture Henri might have taken.

Early summer light, bright but not blinding,
warm but not hot. It went through me,
tinting my mind like wine through water.

My vision created frames as I walked,
keeping violent emotions at bay,
where what seems threatening
can be studied from an inner distance,
like the way one walks around a sculpture
to view it from all angles.

No matter how tenuous I think are the ties
that bind me to the miserable past,
I am not deceived;
heartstrings can be played on,
and twist and tighten
at a moment's notice,
like a devilish phylactery
strangling the life out of me.

Surprising the pain that endures
or perhaps not strange—
enmeshed in desperate, unequal trials
I had no chance of winning,
I buried my feelings so deep
I couldn't find them
and turned my heart to stone,
that slowly is softening.

APERTURE

Behind glass I watch the sky glutted with grackles
circling above an open field. A cluster breaks
from the mass and lands in bare branches
of a nearby hickory. One bird squawks and flaps
as another impinges on his perch. Seconds after settling
into tense suspense they swoop in one wave and plunge
black beaks in rain-sogged earth.

Though I lift my zoom lens again and again, I never
catch their synchronized rise or descent. Cannot fathom
how the connected current of fed bellies must feel
to lift off, wings wide, and rejoin the fold lipping
the bowl of sky. Do their jet bodies tremble as mine?

I cannot leave the glass door or lower the camera,
remembering how I tried in vain to capture breaching
whales in Alaskan waters on our last trip together.
Just look, you said. Your face, empty of hair
and chemo-pale, drank in the fluid black in livid
sea, and I knew what I was frantic to frame.

DANCE IN THE CITY

When I decided to marry you, I was in the cemetery
at Montparnasse. A cloudy Paris day, the black-and-
white faces of the dead stared at no one
under plastic sheaths. Sartre's horizontal slab
lay like a clean white page while Baudelaire's obelisk
claimed a corner: *Pray for us.*

I knew my muscled heart would one day be locked
in this granite metropolis, with its cobblestone paths,
high walls and avenues named to direct the living
to the dead. Life suddenly seemed a slow descent to stone.
But you offered a way out, guiding me to another garden,
where we'd push old earth up and away.

In the abbey-town of Fontevraud, we lay in the medieval night,
our *lune de miel*, a black so complete it masked our open eyes.
In a few hours, the baker would drive past in his wagon,
baguettes sticking out the back, bread for prisoners
whose release a decade earlier transformed the abbey-prison
to monument, men who chose to stay, whose bodies still wore

the blue uniform, their faces their crimes.
My white tulle and satin hid the crimes familiar to me.
At our wedding, the dead, close as my lace stroking the red
church aisle, chanted: Lovrien's breakdown over Grandfather's
affair. Great-Uncle's Depression-era suicide.
My father soon dead from drink.

All my life, I read their lives like so many required
tragedies, the twists to come or avoid. We were like
that painting by Renoir, me creamy fragile in your arms,
you all black poise. Music and color blotted out their voices
and we danced. Anniversary after anniversary. I tell
the dead to return to their tombs, but they won't,
they want our breath, they call it inspired.

SOTTO VOCE

A friend of mine woke up next morning with no voice, which
   temporarily made him technically aphasic, a little thread of
   a hoarse voice like you have after a tonsillectomy, when
   you say, more ice cream, please.
Or when you're lying under a pile of bodies in a mine collapse,
   an earthquake, a car bombing.
Or you didn't get there first in the scramble for the goods, got
   an elbow in the eye from the one ahead, which meant your
   children would be shorter down the line, and theirs, and
   theirs.
He walked missing his voice and wondered what if it didn't
   come back, or if it would be different, authoritative, like
   those radio / TV announcers whose voice is chattel.
So right then he vowed that if his voice did come back he
   would try his damndest to speak for people as he was then.
Cynicism crept into his heart.
He thought: "I could rent out my voice to temporary aphasics
   'cause there's not much money in the permanent aphasic
   community."
Fortunately, he regretted such thoughts and became a bleeding
   heart again, but it didn't help his voice, which never did
   come back.
Now he and literally millions upon millions of the voiceless—
   temporary, permanent, honorary, abject, congenital,
   situational, economic, political—are searching like
   Diogenes for an honest voice, in the desert too, it turns out.

FILCHED

Is that vintage? they ask.

It was my dad's, I say, and think of a thirsty man for whom that word
meant only a crack about drink, *Gimme a tall one of your finest vintage!*

I found it among tie pins and cufflinks in his top drawer, filched it years
before I knew the word,

> when I thought only that I wanted something beautiful
> and ruined,

> something I could take from him who knew work and the
> bar better than home.

Crystal scratched, leather dry and stitching frayed, he never
noticed it was gone, or else he never said.

From his dresser to the carved wooden box of tattered treasures
I buried inside my hand-me-down chest,

> until the no more of him sent me rooting for some relic
> I could hold.

Glass polished and gears set right, new band strapped to my wrist.

Vintage?

It's beautiful, they say.

It was my dad's, and I let them assume, inheritance or gift,

    that he was a man of taste who shared it with his son.

Let others believe I was offered what I stole.

TRIMMING BACK
THE BURNING BUSH
AT BILL BRONK'S

                                        Say,
this one had overgrown its place
by being rooted here.
Or that what had risen to, and over the porch
might bring it down.
Worried the electric lines;
threatened the house within with an inner dark.
                        Yet, better,
say it was the sun's own over-reaching-arch
toward the clearer light, for the greater clarity,
I did what you asked.

It was a bloodless fall with little ornament.

Warmed, as I had to the task,
losing these few remaining *drupes*:
stoney seeds enclosed beneath the scarlet poise
of their fruit's *arils.*
            That inner perdurable,
that second skin, living presence of the future-past
hung on those tributary forms.
In forming November's air
among the deeper shadows
of your greater trees.

This *euonymous,*

slender branches

described in my botany as *alate,* or winged.

In the language of the body,

double spined, almost cruciform

as if lacking the flesh for the perfection of the round.

But once cut back, as you might have said,

to its singular source, becomes the stronger

for being made more stark, if a more severe calligraphy: the god

pollarded.

Or the voice of the god

brought forth out of the self's own wilderness,

now read as the blackened bones

of a possible fire.

Now as fingers pleading

for a hand to stop,

or, if not to stop, to get on with it

and let there be no end.

I would

have cleared the lot of every twig,

had you but wished, off every tree

to make it bare.

Not barren,

but a bare light for you to see

the more of me.

A naked light the dark might take

to shine.

O,

I know you know its will

wills all grow back

in time.

Our graven winter solitary before us,

roots tapped into its own summering

embers banked against the cold,
must hold, or wither
and die
                              out:
first here, then there the greeny sprout,
when next profusion's spring
breaks out.

*drupe: In botany, a stone fruit having a hard nut-like inner
part surrounded by a fleshy or fribrous outer layer.*

aril: In botany, a term applied to coverings or appendages of seeds.

*euonymous: a genus of 170 small trees and shrubs, of which the
common ornamental landscape plant the burning bush is a member
(euonymous atropurpurea). Has small crimson capsules, or drupes.
Leaves turn bright red in fall*

alate: having the appearance of wings.

PILGRIM SOUL

Do observations of fields and mountains,
recorded as the moment permitted
and made under a compulsion
not to forget accidental associations,
reveal some purposive alignment of worlds
within worlds, worlds at right angles or colliding
with the world of my experience?

Such faith in a grand design
has lead to unredeemed violence.
It has stained cathedrals with the gore
of innocents and saints. To follow these threads today,
if you keep paring away at the substance,
might finally, by means of the very mechanics of deliberate
          attention,
produce an unexpected pattern of micro-fractures
          on a surface,
a confluence without meaning. Call this momentary brilliance
          "joy," if not "hope,"
that small burst of light on the edge
          of a newly formed synapse
of the active intelligence. It might produce
a slippery friction, a discharge.

In the middle of my sleep, a voice calls my name with
                    familiar force,
"Donald!" Can it really be my muse, one of my wives, my
        child, my mother?
Are the police about to descend through the moonlight like
        ravening hawks?
This pilgrimage does not map the constraints of geography
or the secrets of my heart.
It follows tracks,
laid down by a mangy bear
who dreams through underbrush.

THE ORGAN BUILDER

So many nights I've listened to the fugue
that filled his shop to keep his world alive,
as if his long-unfinished masterpiece
of pinewood pipes and maple stops gave birth
to strands of Bach, the music of my childhood
all around me, amniotic, rising,

falling, echoing the falling, rising
in my chest, a fugue within a fugue
that stuns me back into a wide-eyed child
who watches how he works the grain, a live
unfurling from the hand plane's throat, a birth.
Light glistens round him like a caul as piece

by piece he shapes his growing masterpiece
while I work, too, a rickety music rising
from my hammer, ringing in the birth
of current running father to son, a fugue
in my fingertips, a hum of whims alive
in the body of an organ builder's child.

The hammer slips, shattering my childhood.
I sink in darkness, grasping for a piece
of pine, my father's callused hand alive
and hauling me toward light, our bodies rising
to the surface where we hear a fugue
composed by two entwined, another birth,

104

our blood inseparable as hands that birth
the pipes as one, no longer man and child
but craftsmen conjuring a centrifuge
of sound. We lean against the bench and piece
together ivories, cathedrals rising
in the thrill of blood, the instrument alive

inside our shop and rising, current live
in every vein, ecstatic for the birth.
The shop is shot with sun, reborn and rising,
catching on a flue, each pipe a child
who turns and lights the next, a masterpiece
of finished wood, a contrapuntal refuge

wrapping round us, peaceful as the birth
of shining flue pipes, all our fugal children
alive and rising, rank on rank, to sing.

POEM FOR ROBERTO BOLAÑO (1953 — 2003)

in the dream fragments
of images gather
and condense, contract

your figure emerges
then suddenly stops
a red shirt, jacket
the color of jade,
glasses that frame eyes
as radiant suns

you greet me with smiles,
no introduction
we know each other
how can this be, R.?
i've read your books and
you've been dead six years

maybe you saw me
as my eyes gazed down
on your words, pages
like paned-glass
through which the author
watches his reader
as he constructs faith
line by line by line

as the dream went on
you decided to live
up the street from me
in a house painted
in red and jade tones
like your quirky clothes

roberto, you're close
like a good neighbor
each day I'll visit
do you read me? good
we will be fine friends
come by whenever

you already do, ghost,
author, companion

help me build a porch
for my citadel
a new addition
to my home you built
long before we met

GARDEN OF STARS

David. David. Francisco
Calls from the dark.
He has risen with intention.
He calls again, his voice
Closing in on my door.

When I last heard him
Use this tone
They took him away,
And he told me
He might die.

I raised my hand to quiet him
But he persisted:
Don't worry, David,
A dead author sells well.

Come, he urges now, and
I, too, rise in the night,
Blindly follow the presence
Of this old Chilote man
Borne by the sea.

He leads me through the dark
Channels and turns of his home.
We take a northern course
Down the hallway as I sight
The belt of his robe
Trailing him like a life line.

We enter a bedroom
That by day abounds
With light and air
Books and Beethoven,
But tonight is black
And quiet like a song of death.

A quadrangular opening
Emerges before us,
The window pushed out
All the way toward the Andes.
I see Francisco's face
Next to mine.

He points out Venus, Mars,
Orion's Betelgeuse,
Speaks of his own
Twenty-eight constellations.
Needing no sextant
He brings me stars
I will never see
In my own land.

We lean on the sill,
Against each other,
And watch the sky.
David, he whispers
Into the silence,
This is my garden of stars.
It is the only thing
That keeps me alive.

J A C K

and I used to ramble in the wasteland behind the Lake St. factory,
seeking Sgt. Gott, our liberator. He was off to the war in Korea.
It was a fable like Parsifal.
Clack clack, a stick, beating the wire fence.
Another stick, cut from an alder, jumped and dodged like an animal
    on a leash,
hopping as it bumped the cracks in the walk.
Jack's aunt, he said, had buried a cat
in the garden with the vertical Madonna bathtub shrine.
Or was it his brother?
When the sleigh passed down Hollis Street, the hard candies rained
    on the pavement
like grenades
and fingers were bent and bruised.
My sister wanted to murder me.
In the yard of the bakery,
the electric cars went in circles all night. There was a crash
and one turned over, its motor screeching like a maimed horse.
The policeman chased us home like cops and robbers
into the tenements of humiliation and poverty.
My dad had yellow teeth.
His mother sold cigars.
Our Lithuanian neighbor gathered crate wood
from the different grocery stores on Main Street
and transported it home in a Radio Flyer wagon.
He broke it into bundles and stored them in the yard.
To me he was the same old man Mike who threw furniture around
    before a storm.

The barber kept his black Cadillac in a rented space in the horse barn.
There was also a hearse.
Joe Bedard was a muscular locomotive mechanic who strolled home
    from Union Station
stripped to his singlet, like a wrestler, black from head to foot with
    machine oil.
He could not raise his arm to comb his hair.
Like my father, I have one eye.
Shadows still surprise me, confusing fact and fiction.
Somewhere in a sandpit famous for rattlesnakes
are the pods of deserted boxcars, rusting into the chemical breeze.
A world transfixed in suspended dust,
a metallic throb in the jaw.
Night winds carried emanations from the cellar,
mold and damp coal and kerosene, wildly sprouting potatoes with
    lavender tentacles.
My father dreamed that showgirls
danced in the alley.
Ti-Jean was not a happy man.

THE MARLEYS OF KINGSTON

—for Hettie Jones

She lays her mouth on his.
He lays his mouth on hers.
They drink each other's hunger and thirst,
spill songs into each other's mouth.

Alleluia.

He spills daughters and sons.
They all need to be nursed—
the six she bears and a few
whose mothers are strangers.

Alleluia

There are mercies in Babylon—hard work, hits,
a Hope Road house. There are evils—
anger and absence, politics
and guns—he takes his bullet; she takes hers.
It stops short of her brain, trapped in a thicket of dreads.

I and I gonna be all right.

Then, thirsty crab crawls into his foot,
drinks every cell of him
except the Alleluia spilled on his children and all
over the world.

Our Sister's singing still.

112

GODSPEED
—for John and Annie Glenn

During his first orbit, I lay
in a hospital bed, wrapped
in a piano concerto by Brahms
which someone had turned on
by accident, my black-haired son
bundled in his cart, caught up
in the first of wordless dreams
he would never learn to compromise,
while an Ohio-born traveler
circled our adventure with his own.

When we met him years later,
stumping Ohio in the seventies,
he crinkled his eyes and said
I looked like Annie. She told me
they ate by candlelight every night,
even if it was only hot dogs.

Last week my son, late bloomer,
weightless with euphoria, married
the girl he said he had to have,
and today the old astronaut,
launched safely again into space,
comments on the beauty of Hawaii,
where perhaps the honeymooners
find a moment to shield their eyes
and scan the sky.

On my refrigerator, a clipping—
Annie brave in a pale hat,
her balding husband's hand
on her shoulder, reminder
that all adventurers who soar
must then descend, survive
the terrors of re-entry, and find
their footing on this common ground.

THE FARMER GORED BY HIS BULL

In memory of Mr. Len Carlson, who died December 22, 1965,
on his farm in Glen Valley, British Columbia

Golden one, that thrust you gave that first
Slipped through my heart caught me by surprise
And held me there, listening to the burst
Of veins feeding a warm flood on the rise.
So many changes now—your black-tipped horn
Turned red, my soul turned free, my wondering eyes
Wide open everywhere. My body, shorn
Of weight and years, is just a visitor,
Joined by a silvery thread with this newborn
Beast we have made, our coupled minotaur—
A bull's head hoists the body of a man!
I know your labyrinth, unraveler;
Below, the world lies open to my scan—
I see how all that ended first began.

So strange, that I who raised you from a calf
Have now been raised by you! You tossed me high
To lay me low—I wonder, should I laugh
To see what comes to pass, or should I cry?
We were meant for a time when danger bound
To beauty made that beauty multiply.
I saw the way those pointed glories crowned
Your head, lit up your eyes, sparked a wild beat
That set your black hooves stamping on the ground.
To cut them, burn their roots, would bring defeat

To both of us—without his horns a bull
Is half without his sex, left incomplete,
And I, I would have missed the miracle
Of seeing you so strong and beautiful.

But still, I pierced you first. I shoved that steel ring
Clean through your nostrils, clamped and locked it there,
Locked the surging strength of the tawny yearling
To human will, and made you so aware
That strength will yield to pain—yes, where I led
You followed, though your nostrils still might flare.
While I could hold you, many times instead
I let you loose to prance across the field
With horns that dazzled every cow you bred
And harried shadow rivals, made them yield
To you, my minotaur! Oh, we were friends
At play this wintry day when you unreeled
The silvery thread and showed me as it ends
Strength sometimes bends, but beauty rends, it rends!

K E N N Y S P E A K S

The priest who saved a boy from terror knew.
I can guess now he was angry about "hell"
and a boy who believed all he was told.
Father stood in his black cassock like a magician
plucking a quarter from behind a kid's ear,
gently, he said, "Listen. To me. You
can do nothing worthy of hell, yours
is a scrupulous conscience." In 1954
in Chicago, I was freed to fall asleep and hope
to wake and find me still on earth, a boy.

As an adult, I faced a kid who sat
in my classroom staring at his teacher,
and could not speak at all. Opened,
his mouth made syllables, squeaks
other kids learned to recognize.
But if his hell was a tongue melted
in some furnace he'd survived, he did,
write two stories. "You could be good at this,"
I told him, having no cassock, Roman collar,
or magic coin to offer, just words with which
the thing can be offered which
is then accepted or refused and
so it must have been.

28 AUGUST 1833.
CALLED UPON MR. WORDSWORTH

28 August 1833. Called upon Mr. Wordsworth.
His daughters called him in & he sat
Across from me in goggles, speaking with
The greatest simplicity, mainly of America,
A society he deemed enlightened by
A superficial tuition out of all proportion
To its being restrained by morality –

Schools do no good. He spoke
Of Newton's law as though
It were to be overturned. He said "what
Is needed most in America
Is civil war to teach them the necessity
Of tying tighter the social bonds."
America's vulgarity, he insisted, is a result

Of its pioneer state, yet the world
Is too much with them, there is a lack
Of class among men of leisure.
Outside, in his garden, the place
Where he wrote his thousands of lines,
I look into his red & sour eyes
That no longer read words,

& since he writes no prose
His head carries a book's worth of verse
From which he freely quotes & it seems
So new, you'd think he'd newly improvised.
We'd walked over a mile, stopping
Every hundred paces or so
For him to quote a verse. His opinions
That of an old man who never aged past seventeen.

HARMONY, USA

Fog rolls in off Moro Bay, a heavy,
churning motion—and we are in it.

Road signs can't be seen. The sun a dim fuse.
Each curve surprises, then is gone, just our headlights

on fog, its swirling generosity
as now it swings open to windswept cliffs,

gulls and cormorants beyond. No horizon.
No retaining that distinction. Gun-grey swells

curl up from unseen depths, rise huge
against the cliffs, leave scrawls of brine arcing

up shore. The salt-scaled trunk of a fig tree
glints where light now touches. From the bluff,

pelicans drop bodily into surf, emerge
with fish wriggling in their gullets—a moment

not expected, never meant, as fog rolls closed,
our lights thrown back into our own faces.

We let ourselves be printed,
frisked and scanned, filled out forms, and still weren't sure
they'd let us see my nephew, till a light
blinked, a buzzer sounded, a heavy bolt
dropped; then a huge metal door hissed open

to a long, narrow room with low ceiling,
rows of plastic chairs bolted to the floor,
prisoners sitting under glaring lights
with wives, girlfriends and families,
their children playing in a big sandbox
beneath a primitive mural with cliffs,
gulls rising and dipping into low fog,
enormous orange sun above the horizon.

Then Robert was led in. His close-cropped hair,
grey, receding, surprised me, but not the dark,
intense eyes and dimpled chin of the boy
I used to babysit. Faded workshirt
and jeans. Worn-out tennis shoes. When we sat,
he kept looking beyond us, left and right,
then into our eyes to see behind him.

The guy behind me's a snitch. The other's
a friend, but we don't talk out here. Goonies
hear everything, write you up just for kicks.
You wanna know what it's like doin' time?
We march single-file, arm's length apart.
Always some goony's face up close or watching
through a window. Same routine every day.
A number determines what mail you get,

what books you read, who you sit by at meals.
7, noon and 5. Tin trays with runny
mush or mashed potatoes, cold peas and spam
all in its right place. Nights, one bare bulb for
twelve of us. We can pound the walls, yell, or jack-off
in silence. Some nights a needle gets through
and we're in heaven. Nothing you'd notice.

Some guys get catalogues or girly-mags
to keep them dreaming. Me, I keep busy
cleaning—I do what I have to—windows,
urinals, goonies' boots, even their pickups
in the parking lot. Some days I can feel
someone else inside my body. I'm sweeping
or standing in steam from the dishwasher
and he'll shout, Eat shit, Goonies! He waltzes
where he wants, masturbates in well-lit rooms,
strolls into that mural you're looking at,
flies with gulls way beyond the horizon.
So, tell me, what's it like out there these days?

This morning at the motel she showered.
I watched Phil Donaghue with some trustee
from Texas describing how he was attacked
by a pack of bloodhounds as the warden
and other officials looked on. Folding
jeans then shirts, I thought in turn of chasing
and being chased: first a ridgeback bounding
up a slope, catching the scent on a clump
of stinkweed, along a dusty creek-bed.
Then the prisoner, stumbling rock to rock

across scree, the baying close. They caught me
in a ravine. I rose, fell, turned and rose
again, hounds hanging from my crotch and chest . . . .

The warden asked Donaghue, "Who you gonna
believe, a law enforcement officer
or this con?" I switched the TV off just as
the trustee lifted his shirt to show us
his scars, saw them shrink to a fading dot
as she, naked, stepped out through steam.

*Should've seen the wedding we had once.
Youd've loved the bride, spiked hair, plump, a real
beauty, Here Comes the Bride on the intercom*

*as she slowly marched through the open door
in a long flowing gown, the groom a friend,
a Mongol doin' time here for arson.*

*Should've seen us cons in clean blues, happy
as cons could be, goonies shooting photos
as if we all was family. All the Mongols*

*from LA were here, wearing shiny suits,
standing with the judge under a flowered
arch. We all clapped when she put on his ring,*

*stuffed our faces with cake, waited in line
to congratulate the bride. Damn goonies
wrote me up for touching her veil—hell,*

I just wanted to see her face. She ran
under a hail of rice, waved as she left,
waved and waved, long after the door hissed closed.

Past Ragged Point—zebras. I count twelve grazing
just off the road. stripes pale against the fog.

Other cars have stopped, couples and families
leaning over the fence, snapping photos,

stretching to touch the one closest. We wedge
in with the others, wondering who would bring

zebras from their vast savannah rangelands
to this windswept, fogbound corner of coast,

when the horses from childhood come to mind:
Flicka, Silver, Trigger, Beucephalus,

all the Shetlands on cereal boxes,
wild stallions I raced through backyard grass.

These days there's only one horse left, an angry
Lipizon pounding hard against his stall

when a body I want, can't have, walks past.
I'm calm on the surface, but that Lipizon

keeps on kicking, long after the moment
has passed. Now he's a lion in tall grass

sniffing the air as I lean close to read
the lines of their coats for some hint they know

he'll pounce, tear open their soft underbellies,
chew their entrails in the warm savannah

dusk. Ears flicker. Muscles ripple. We're all
leaning, breath mixing, grazing on zebras.

When you leave they'll make us strip, shine flashlights
up our asses, stick a gloved finger in
to grope for pills and knives. You should see us
leaning into the wall, our butts a row of . . .

of what, Uncle, you're the poet—puckered
lips? Little kisses? A line of moonflowers,
each with its own aroma? How 'bout stars,
a whole constellation waiting for goonies

to finish? They check our hair, shove a flashlight
(the same one) into our mouths, lift our balls.
They know our tricks and we know what they don't—
cons can swallow anything, crap it out

the next day. Still it's night I love the best,
the other guys asleep. I touch my body
like no other can, go first to forehead,
lips, dimpled chin, along my neck, then stroke

chest to hip, like a woman would, but no
woman fits these fantasies. I touch thighs,
shins, calloused soles. This ain't about jack'n
off (that's for later, quick, in shower steam);

it's me claiming my body back, the man,
whatever he's become. I never touch
my asshole, though. Goonies own it, like words,
everything we do in daylight. They keep us

bent like that for an hour, write us up
if someone farts or groans or hasn't stooped
enough. Uncle, would you bend, spread your cheeks,
let some guard stick a cold finger way in,

jiggle it a bit to see if you get
hard, pull it out real quick? And what'd you call
that row of butts glowing in flashlight beams—
blooming anai? Yeah, but in whose garden?

We made love, then left the motel, driving
back toward the lives we'd left, those fictions we
depend on. I kept thinking: was that warden

on his horse flat or round? I know the currents
rushing through his body—the flow of death
over the flow of life—are in us all,

but that's abstract. He loves his horse without
irony or complication, loves a
clear, simple order. He must be flat or else

he'd wonder at his own inhibited
pity. Not that I would call the dogs off,
set a fellow sufferer free, the image

too rich for that—a bloodied archetype,
Actaeon, no doubt, in love with the dreaded
goddess, his own hounds clawing out his eyes

to lay them at her naked feet. The woods
were beautiful that day, so full of life
amid the dying leaves and rotting ferns

his horse was chewing to fuel its blood. He must
be flat or else he'd go from doubt to want,
outrage to certainty, and feel at times,

in a deep embrace, another's current. Yet
he must be round or else the flood within
or the flood without would wash him away.

Thinking that way, the motor pinging low,
I began to sympathize with the warden,
had him lift the trustee from the ravine,

set him running again. His horse? I would've
pushed her over, but that mare kept tugging
at the ferns, getting rounder and rounder.

I'm breaking the rules, I know, by talking
to you. So you can find me through the fog
I write *zebra*. He raises his head as if
to speak: what wisdom, you might ask, leaning

over the page, lips moving, could come
from a body that's a parody of
convict, horse and text, a sign for all three
shifting according to strict laws? I've seen
Egyptians with eyes like his, ebony
set in darker rings, detached from the moment,
like that elevator operator in Cairo
who held the door open and beckoned me
in with a quick, unexpected, *Thank you.*

Since I've stepped into that infinity
of desire between us, let me confess
I love you, oh, I want you. I would enter
your spinning mind, impose on your attention
the figure you've always wanted: the object
itself, without *it*, without *self*. I'd be
You in an instant, if you'd let me
and even if you wouldn't. Always shifting,
never touching, in the prison-house
of language we're all innocent. . . .

                                    But, hey, you
stopped reading. Bored? Confused? Or did your body
feel a message, so you went to relieve
yourself of that significance? Pity.
When you left the zebra talked up a storm,
let us ride him, took pictures of us
with our own cameras, heard you coming so
went back to silence. Focusing again,
ignore the golden stream arcing toward
his feet, steam mixing with fog. It's his lips
I want you to see. They're moving. They're saying,

Thank you.

Words? Hell. They're all so meaningless. There was
that three-holer in a Motel 6 in
Yuba City. She touched me when she talked,

liked my chin. So I switched off the lights, did
what comes natural. Next I knew she was
tied to the bed, naked, not breathing. Body

did it. Went to work with hips and tongue. Felt
soothed after. I helped her with her torn blouse,
found her panties under the bed . . . . I'm innocent.

We all are. Us drugstore robbers, fire-
starters, public poisoners and loud-mouthed
pimps. The truth be known, you'd be here with us.

Both of you. No rays detect your guilt,
nor count the ways you done dirt. Now I've gone
and scared you. Damn. Do you like the mural?

Did it myself. I know, the sun's too big,
waves all off, no perspective to speak of;
still, a place I'd love to be. No words there,

no cons, their ten thousand stories. I never
finished mine: Whoever locked the door did it
from inside, easy to step out into

the August night. Junebugs banging a globe.
Old Colusa Road. Then sirens. Flashing
lights, my face slammed to the dirt by cops

cuffing me. So, Uncle, tell me, am I
some animal, caged to reflect on guilt?
Fuckin' words, that's all. Mine against all theirs.

The highway lines rush past. What we desire
we leave behind. I see the fading light
and gauge my feelings for this woman sleeping
beside me, stroke her hair and point the car
away from maximum security.

The motor's hum is not my heart, nor speed,
nor temperature. I smell the ocean air
rushing into this inland valley: man
and woman and such a gap between us
we'll never fill it, though our passion tries.

We both laughed at the sign—*Absolutely*
no prisoners allowed inside the children's
sandbox. I watched a con's young daughter tamp
elaborate walls around a castle, saw
her frightened eyes when she looked toward me.

If I were up for life, would my companion
slip a blade inside the sand, or carve a message
beyond that small square window where
conscience still comes to view the ones it loves,
Help me, before this man tears me apart?

And if I touch her cheek, will she awake
and smell the air and see the drifting fog,
and understand the highway's lines are here
to tell us when to pass and where to merge?

130

In last night's dream the cons were women dressed
as zebras, kissing me and tearing me
apart. I was the groom, the sacrifice,
my head impaled and planted in the sand,
singing out my *O* with a country twang.

Jerusalem the Bride. I saw her on
TV dressed in a gown of snow, the news:
six old men crushed when a coffee house roof
caved in, their hukkas still in their mouths—
a tragedy you have to sing about.

So, *O*, I cry, as if that vowel were all
I need to get us through the fog, the road's
dips and curves foretold by signs we can't see
as we inch along at fifteen thousand
explosions per second, and below us
the Pacific's unrelenting roar—O,

I'm a liar without a lyre, blinded
by my own headlights, looking deep into
your eyes, Dear Reader, for a pocket
of clarity, a reason to keep going,
at least a sign—just one—for the next town:

BIOLOGICA

DEAD CATFISH

Persistent crone. Your medieval grin,
(evoking Brueghel) settled in the stone
and switchgrass sometime in the summer light
and stayed. The wind refused to throw you back.
The storm last week could not produce the waves
to reach you where you rotted in the shade

and petrified. I recognize this shade
of gray as semi-permanent, your grin,
the rictus in a fevered dream that waves
and floats, as something of a childhood touchstone:
Once a bird, your image filters back
a catfish. Sick hallucinations light

such dreams in much the way that sunlight
draws your shadow where I step. A nightshade
in the day, you cultivate a switchback
atmosphere, a counter-Lohengrin
where hero is enchanter. Where the stone-
cracked stage shall have no magic swan or waves

of celebrants or swords, but tidal waves
of stagnant air; a concrete satellite
in static orbit fixed upon a stone;
a brittle plinth and monument to schaden-
freude. A luckless path. But here's that grin
and mockery of Cheshire Cat! A back-

and-forth along the frissoned razorback
of clowning time, you have the nerve to wave
me down and hold me here, to press your grin
into the mirror of the lakeblue light.
My eyes and yours, behind their carbon shade
of hardened death, are locked like mason's stone

as viral memory corrodes to breakstone
beach. The progress of your broken back
is mimicked in the cloudline where the shade
of crawling afternoon traverses waves
now audible and focuses the light
remaining on your curtain call. You grin

your bottom-feeder grin of stone, inert
and elegant, enlightened, coming back
to life in waves of shade across the dirt.

KOCH'S BONES

A stretched head with
formidable jaws,
a series of ribs forming
a large ovoid body and
the vestiges of flippers
arranged in undulating shape,
one hundred fourteen feet in length,
those bones Dr. Koch
displayed in the Apollo Saloon,
Broadway 1845,
Hydragos Sillimanii, or
Silliman's master-of-the-seas,
its head raised into position –

"Dr. Koch, this must be a hoax.
you may fool the public,
who are of shallow persuasion,
but not the eyes of
a skilled anatomist:
the teeth have double roots,
meaning it's mammal, and
these bones come from
several different skeletons
cunningly arranged into one.
I don't doubt you found
these saurian remains of the
Tertiary Age *Basilosaurus*

in Alabama. Negro slaves
believed them to be
the bones of fallen angels."

Despite the occasional charade,
Koch was no charlatan.
Removing flints from the bones
of mastodons and giant sloths
he proved that man had lived
in North America centuries
before Columbus. Koch
despaired of a world
composed wholly of reason,
the often damning and
indifferent nature of which
at times cannot be reconciled

CATALOG OF BIRDS

Galapagos Archipelago, September

We know of three birds classified as thrushes
on these Islands. All American.
Three owls, a hawk, some other carrion-
devouring Polybori. But the rushes
chime with a cacophony of finches!
Gradients of *Geospiza*, sleek
and differentiated by the beak,
all black and brown from 5 to 7 inches.
Starling-faced and parrot-faced, the birds
demark an evolutionary route,
a mixed race in a ring of cul-de-sacs.
The finches leave the mocking thrush without
a quick reply, confused and lost for words,
confronted with a sense of what she lacks.

THE LAST MARLIN

Captain Brad says

-In the 30's they stacked Marlin
on the dock in Bimini like cord wood

> Hemingway could've loaded a truck
> with blue fin he reeled through
> marauding sharks
> > machine gunned
> > to protect his catch

now all these creatures are scarce
and we must push south
from Cat Island

> to Concepcion
> before someone hooks the last marlin
> in Pinas Bay...

casting off the bow line
a sweet breeze blowing from the mangrove
contains all there is to know

I take the world into my lungs
and expel it

every breath
the beginning and
end of tiny insects
large mammals

my chest expands to hold
the late Pleistocene
and all five extinctions
that precede it

WHAT THE ELEPHANTS ARE DOING

Elephants often bury the dead,
including dead elephants,
other dead animals they find,
and even dead humans
they have killed.
They cover the bodies
with earth and vegetation.
A group of scientists and park officials
working on a cropping scheme
in Uganda collected the ears and feet
of the dead elephants
to sell later for making
handbags and umbrella stands,
and put them in a shed.
One night a group of elephants
broke into the shed
and buried the ears and feet.
—found poem from *Portraits In The Wild*, Cynthia Moss, 1975

Blessed are the buriers,
for theirs is the kingdom of dust.
At night, the elephants enter
even the tiniest cubbies
of the dreamhouse,
hearing themselves calling
for themselves
from the remains:
O ears, harken.
O feet, find the way.

They answer in behemoth dark,
working silently, though their heat
sets fire to huts.

Under the moon
their vast undertaking, their
ponderous requiem,
raises a cloud of dust
that from far off looks like storm,
the approach of all souls.

Their bodies sway back and
forth, back and
forth, wrinkled caravans of blame

and recollection,
their ears grand sails

STARVELINGS

(Or, the Woods and the Wide, Wide World)

The sun's a color control knob gone kaput,
turning on only a monochrome day.
The far woods are eroding into lime,
the nearer barely stir. Stark, black limbs cut
no capers,
        as starvelings too worn out to play
endure in last rags till a bitterer time,
and millions gasp, in sound bites, at the plight
of junior stoics too numb to despair,
at apathetic children hosting flies

as trees host birds. The same quick appetite
probing cracks in bark, nuthatches share

with flies that salivate round nostrils, eyes.

Dear God! Please bear with us till tomorrow's
normal service brings its norm of sorrows.

S E E D

Bridge to birth, ancient vessel of present form,
mute determination packed tight
in a tidy valise, she waits with the patience
of redwoods or a stone for water,
ready with immortality, botany's cockroach.

Determined in her habit like a music box,
until an unsprung zone releases
the winged snake that riles itself up
toward the orb that billows light
as though to devour it.

If we carried a seed in our pockets,
if we'd be messengers who walked
the clear paths to then and survived
with fruit, who were bland and wooly
with our bristles and buckteeth,
with information, clogged with mud and roots
that kept bringing us down to the ground
made us slow, puddles and ruts that fill with rain
our sister, the weeds that hold us,
pine cone and horizon, we'd cherish moss
humming to the bark, and to river beds
strewn with pluming currents, and we'd sit
beside the gravel as it popped in the heat.

And we'd understand crows laughing,
live safe in the embrace of elements,
grateful to the seed for guidance.

COSMOLOGICA

I BELIEVE

I believe in a city that
Talks to itself a city
With three faces like
The dancers that come home at dawn
Three cities and a river and
A false light in the eye of the poor
Where love comes down from
The roof tops at noon
And is greater than the sum
Of its pieces

MEETING MAMMOTH CAVE, EIGHT MONTHS PREGNANT

With my dark eyes open,
I search into the dark
for a reassurance
to soothe me like a look.

No beam will sink or angle,
no slow new mineral drip
through the circling ceiling,
no change of quiet drop.

A womb will throw me outward
(unbreakably deep kiss),
inhospitable, solid,
into no circumference,

carrying dark to hold me,
to empty the slippery
solid cavern's holding,
to hollow the beautiful

loud strength of a darkness
only dark can reassure,
in the night to my humanness
the unparticled has poured.

MENDEL CONSIDERS THE MOON

My hair seems
Whiter in lamplight. The flame flickers
Good fortune over and over – and for what?
                                                                    - Tu Fu

All these years I was
waiting for God
to move in me

until I took flight,
was pollen, was rough seed
tossed by wind,
carried on bee underbellies,

until I was part of the circle
that holds everything,

waiting
until I took root.

Here, I am stamen, pistil, stem,
petal unfurling, azalea,
white mass of flowers
fragrant under the moon.

B R

Viscous, dark red, volatile, foul-smelling non-metal. Besides mercury, it is the only element that is liquid at room temperature. Density: 3.1g/cm³. Its name comes from *bromos*, stench in Greek. It was discovered by the Frenchman Antoine-Jérôme Balard in 1826.

Bromine is very reactive: it attacks and disolves gold; burns aluminum, titanium and mercury; explodes with white phosphorus and potassium. Paradoxically, however, it can also be used as an inhibitor against the burning of clothes, furniture and electronic items. Exposure to its vapors reduces sexual activity. This was first noted when it became a complaint in workers who inhaled excess bromine in factories where it was made.

Bromine is concentrated in marine snails with spiral shells of the genus *Murex*. A purple dye, which is a compound of bromine, can be extracted from these snails. This dye is mentioned in the Bible, for example in the Second Book of Moses and the Book of Ezekiel, and was used for coloring the robes of Roman emperors.

Belousov and Zhabotinsky discovered an oscillating chemical reaction in the Soviet Union in the 1950s. The oscillations occur via reactions of bromine compounds in the following manner. In an "eruptive" or "autocatalytic" reaction, bromous acid increases by the fact that the number of molecules doubles in each reaction step. This increase in bromous acid causes oxidation of the ion Br+2 (red) to Br+3 (blue), the latter generating bromide. Bromide then consumes the bromous acid and thus stops the "eruption". Thereafter the process restarts, as small amounts of bromous acid, which is produced by a pool of bromate, increase eruptively again. If the solution is not stirred, blue spiral or concentric waves appear on a red background.

35 BROMINE

The spiral of the snail.
The purple tone
in Ezekiel's voice.
The togas
of the noblemen.

The snail's oblation:
an unceasing
dance.
Bromous acid
gives birth to itself.
The spiral
rotates.
Red turns blue.
Bromide is born.
Blue turns red.
Bromous acid
decays.
Bromate renews it.
The spiral
keeps turning.

It's the dance
of the noble glow.
The one
that destroys
jewelry,
resists
fire,
snuffs out
sex.

It's the dance of spirals,
of imperial snails,
pregnant with color,
loaded
with bromine,
pregnant
with stench.

T M

Silvery-gray metal. Density: 9.32 g/cm³. In 1879, the Swedish Per Teodor Cleve found that erbium oxide was contaminated by this element. Theodore William Richards, Nobel Prize winner in 1914, isolated it in 1911 from thulium bromate after fifteen thousand recrystalizations. The name comes from *Thule*, a mythical name for Scandinavia.

It is the least common of the "rare earths" (elements No. 57 to No. 71), in which inner electron shells are filled with increasing atomic number.

Irradiation of the isotope thulium-169 with neutrons in a reactor produces thulium-170. The latter emits X-rays from portable boxes with no electronics and no electrical supply. These boxes are widely used, namely in archeology to inspect sites before digging, in medicine, in the control of interior parts of machines, and in police investigations. The half-life of this X-ray emission is 129 days.

69 THULIUM

Minks in tunnels,
bones in graves,
money in jars:
I have a lamp of Thulium,
the rarest
of all rare earths.

I can see your marrow,
things
in your suitcase.
I can see
your heartbeat.

My lamp of Thulium
lights you up
inside,
shows all of you
where you
are not.

THE ZIGZAG OF LIGHT

Blue waves,
the shortest,
struggle most
when they encounter
water droplets or
dust. They scatter
then enter
our vision
from different sites.
This is why
the sky
appears blue.

After a storm
if sun emerges
its light is bent
by air's lingering
water the way
it's bent by a prism
balanced
in an open hand.
This is why
we can admire
at times
a rainbow's full fire

and might be why,
knowing, too, the sun's
gases travel up
from its core
and ring the hot star
like a ten
thousand-toned
bell
I'm inclined
towards some
strange faith
as the sun sends
down its distant
harmonies and light

casts fine patterns
on the pock-marked
mountains, grey
factories and trains, on spires
and temples and border
guards, on men
searching through
recycle bins and women
stepping over the gutters'
stones and on the homes
of this street with their dust-
streaked panes and between
the closed slats
of the blinds.

COSMIC THREADS

In the vinyl cells of an ice cube tray,
among the hooks and sinkers,
were bees of Merovingian design
Immortal like the Golden Bream
that grace the Emperor's Pool,
Napoleon at Versailles
or Yu-Huang, the Jade Emperor,
who dims the Milky Way,
the seventh day of the seventh moon.
Who knows the efficacy of the formula
that turns lead to gold
unless she stands back
like Vega in her longing for Altair
and tracks the shadows on the lawn
where bulls decay and spawn
the humble bee?

THE UNIVERSE IS A BEE

The universe is a bee
A small golden thing
Hovering in the midst
Of a great darkness
As if straining
To let there be light
Flickering wings
Throwing off sparks

The universe is a bee
And each eye of the bee is a bee
And each wing is a bee
It is a bee of bees
Each bee the same
With bees for eyes and
Bees for wings and so on
Each spark that flies
From its bee wings
Is a bee of light
A river of light
Is a river of bees

There are bees hidden in the bees
And bees hidden in the honey
Honey hidden in the bees
Hiding in the honey
And hiding in the bees

The bee is a mind serene

That hum you hear now....

    Is the bee
    At the center
    Of everything

In the beginning
Night opened a window
And let out its own light
And called it a bee

Nothing was made
That was made
Without the bee

And the bee said
Let there be hives
And there were hives
And the bee saw
That they were good

There are bees hidden
In the mountains
Among the cliffs
Hives hidden in the trees
And hives hidden
In the ground
And in the rocky places
And in the walls
There is honey hidden
In the mountains and
Among the caves
Hidden in the ground
And in many places

The bee is a mind
That moves in beauty

The universe is a bee
That hovers above
That dark flower
Taking what it is given
Turning it into light

Oh bee of the universe
Give us the light
Necessary to find
Your dark honey

EKPHRASTICA

WHISTLER'S BLUE / A NOCTURNE

If a man appears alone
on a bridge

on a snowy evening
walking toward

a series of lights
in a row of windows

he doesn't necessarily
have a future

or a past he is simply
a point on a grid

part of a composition
that tells us

what it is
while implying it is

more than it says
we follow him

into the night
because of the blue

we want to know
from whence

he's come and where
he's going

because the blue
envelops

everything but is
thin as air

because it's everywhere
like the nerves

of an acrobat
in pain

and we can hear it
asking us

to shed our skins
and follow

GIRLIE SHOW, 1941

I strut
on his canvas
with three inch silver heels,

my high full breasts,
their mercurochrome
nipples,

my navel
a third eye
looking at men

who hide
in the burlesque theatre's
dark,

my feelings buried
so deep
they will never find them.

Only the drummer
in the orchestra pit,
his head turned from me

to his cymbals and drums,
doesn't care
that I am nude.

NIGHTHAWKS, 1942

The café's bright,
too bright. Henna-haired,
perched on a counter stool,
beside a man
in his wide-brimmed
hat and dark blue suit,
I might as well be alone.
The red tip of his cigarette
burns to ash. I fiddle
with a match cover;
the white-capped counterman
gazes at my neckline.
Empty white
mugs on the counter
wait to be refilled
like my life. I want
my fellow nighthawk
to take my hand,
so near to his,
I want to stroll with him
on the empty town streets,
the night warm
as breakfast oatmeal.
Against the back wall,
two coffee urns,
their vents like eyes,
watch.

DISCIPLE

Frida Kahlo, I have slipped into your cult.
Morning bath is vapor-haze, a tumult:
my feet split like amoebas, mirror themselves
at green-gray water's edge, then meld to Ceibas,
roots teasing death, branches stretched to the sky.

Hubris to imagine I'm your daughter,
that a still-born girl survives. My labor's
crafting dioramas, your face, peach lips
unsmiling, arched brows beneath the midnight braids,
geraniums entwined. Backdrop's yellow,
meaning sickness, meaning joy.

I had you painfully tattooed to my
right thigh, for I could find no rack or screw
to justify my art—perhaps a skeleton
or two. I work with scissors, glitter, glue,

one thin gold star, *recuerdo* of my father,
unschooled Jew who sold insurance, sold
smoked hams. Long ago, I stored his portrait
in the back, heavy jowls and deep-sunk eye,
thinking, *No resemblance*, thinking, *Not my best*.
I paint myself a babe suckling your breast,

in night's embracing kitsch, its altered light.
For diversion, I make pendants of the Virgin
Guadalupe, an adopted saint,
her image a devout, eternal gleaming
on hammered foil. I loop wire to her crown,
thread a red silk choker. Frida Kahlo,

I have built you a small altar, built it over
my lost temple, thick with vines. I burn
pine incense; with a draft, I hope to rise.
And you return my gaze with level eyes.

HUMILIANA: PORTRAIT
IN THE SPARE ROOM

Her smile is so slight
It must have pained her.
Perhaps she did not understand
The camera, or felt betrayed,
Feared what it might take from her.

I can see the edges
Of her lips drop back
To where the world
Would always catch her:

Readying the boat for Pancho
To get to school, taking
Their horse to the small fields,
Plotting for the brief season,
Waiting for a whaling husband
To sail home.

I am lifted to her brown, sad eyes
And I see my aunt Laura, limping
Through the old dining room,
Hauling her leg to the kitchen,
Dragging herself to an early
Cancer death. I hear again
The sister-wail of grief
Force open my mother's mouth
On an early school day,

171

Until Humiliana quiets me,
Brings me back to where it's okay,
Where things need to be done,
Where rings of hair lie against her
Forehead, where her look holds me.

Humiliana. Humble mother
Of Francisco. I come to the spare room
To see you when I'm alone,
See that you have risen
From the earth, and are pure,
Mother to us all.

MICHELANGELO

What a deep torment he was haunted by!
Alone, removed, he raised on the dark wall
Sibyls and Prophets, and above them all
the final judgment streaming from the sky.
Prometheus aspiring too high,
he heard within himself the stubborn call
of country, love and glory and their fall.
He dreamed all die and dreamed that all dreams lie.
Those heavy giants, with their powers drained,
those slaves within unyielding stone constrained,
how in strange shapes he made them twist and thrash;
and in cold marbles where his proud soul flamed,
how with a surge of anger he made flash
a god enraged by matter never tamed!

A L I C E   N E E L
1900-1984

You said the closest that you ever came
to a self-portrait was an empty chair
beside a window. But your sitters, bare
or clothed, could not have felt the same;
they sat for you with all their pride and shame,
prepared to be discovered and to share
themselves because deep down they were aware
you'd show the truth without bias or blame.
Warhol sat for you, naked to the waist,
eyes closed, his body trussed, scarred and defaced,
and cupped his hands, resting in quietude.
And then at 80 finally you sat,
with just a brush and rag and glasses, nude,
fat, flabby, watching us, and that was that.

CALDER IN CONNECTICUT

Liberated, like arrows at the moon,
In hushed expectation they gape
Upward craning, breathing in unison
Unconsciously whispering and gently
Longing to ascend, thinking but a nuance of air
Will animate the great bird's multiplicity.
Il faut l'aimer.
And one wonders why that lover of river
Who soared over Florida, Penn's wood
And this silent stream had not the time
For the iron metaphor, did not tramp round
These spectral snowbound apparitions.
Or seek the libations such Graces casually
Offered, which is to ask why he was
Not other than himself, lonely inventor
Of just such flights, though in truth
His lacked that nice equilibrium,
Snared in the mundane, transmutable
Sphere, wired to words searching proper
Trajectories, vectors, the dynamics
Of mind, place, plant, the rhythms
Evanescent, where favorite black
Was spruce laden with snow and crows
Raked the raucous dawn.

VEL♀CITY

*— Film of President Kennedy, seconds before he was shot,
donated to Dallas museum, February 2007*

See how she turns to the crowds, air blowing her bangs back.
  Their love waving, pink as her nubbled suit and pillbox hat
    edged in black. He savors it too, as if all the pomp
      were some inside joke.

        Some day you might grow up to be president.

His grin says, *It's me, but couldn't it have been anyone
 along the parade route? No, you, you!* All of Dallas responds,
   adoration touching his face, hers. You can see them
     opening like the convertible:

His square head, jacket bunched at neck, her wide delight
  as she turns to the camera. Joy fills their bodies like
    an anesthesia that will fail them.
      There is a prayer that says

        Shield the joyful.

Forty years the filmmaker tried to keep them glad and safe
  in this moment. This hidden reel our own: Where is
    the Kodachrome of before, when does one frame slip
      to the next? *If only, we say, my mother hadn't died,
        my brother run away, or I'd had more help in school.*

          If only I'd married what's-his-name.

176

The perfect vase pulled by gravity to the floor. She once said
  to DeGaulle, *Monsieur le President, my ancestors were French.*
    He bowed, saying, *Mine too, Madame.* My relatives
      would say things like

                Stay as sweet as you are.

I would look at them the way she smiles in this grainy
  and colorful clip, which the networks run three times,
    rolling back to that exact moment:
      How to explain the acceleration forward?

Rick Mullin

2012 Soutine

THE CARCASS OF BEEF

They'd broken through the old brick wall in Castaing's
carriage house, a renovation under way.
Soutine took full advantage of this, casting

chickens in full plumage pendent, gray
and gold and green against a jagged frame
of darkness, squawking in the ecstasy

of death. Talons, beaks and wattles flamed
and sputtered in a nightmare space of murder
on his canvas. A still life series ran to game,

the hare against the green slats of a shutter,
the turkey on a cloth with golden apples.
Soutine conveyed their extremis in color.

Not satisfied, he bartered with his hapless
dealer to procure a side of beef
when he returned to Paris. Butchers grappled

with a battered carcass up the stairs, a brief
comedic interlude at the apartment
he'd been renting. To the hired men's relief

it made it through the door. The painter sent
for Paulette once the butcher's boy had hung
the cage of ribs. His motif was the Rembrandt

at the Louvre, that bleeding carcass strung
upon the rack across a room ... the girl
appearing at the door. But Chaïm would come

a little closer to his model. And he'd hurl
himself at more extensive spans of canvas.
Paulette arrived to find him in a world

of meat, his palette fat with gristle and his
model dripping on the floor. She placed
a pan to catch the blood. "But Chaïm, can this

thing hang here overnight?" Paulette could taste
the painting as the smell of colors mixed
with beef. Apparently the painter faced

another sleepless night. His helper fixed
herself a bed this time, but had to wake
each hour to baste the hulk. "Paulette, the trick's

to keep it bleeding," Chaïm commanded. "Make
it wet." She wetted it. And when the morning sun
came shining through the window, you'd mistake

the carcass for a red Céret, a run-
ning track of bones beneath a sagging skein.
By noon, the horrid greenback flies had come

and Soutine had another canvas pinned
and propped against an oil-splattered table.
He mixed a pile of cobalt and alizarin,

a blackout violet at the center of a scumbled
wheel of colors bleeding into gray.
His oil palimpsest began to bubble

in the heat as Soutine layered splay
on splay of tortured meat between
the scratchwork ribs to end the second day.

And sunrise found him scraping back the green
he'd laid in semidarkness. Hours passed.
The colors changed. The carcass wore a sheen

of viscous rot, its rind a venous blast
of atrophy. It cracked in hieroglyphs
of morbid skin. The painter, slouching, cast

his shadow on the sagging monolith.
By 12 o'clock, the neighbors were amassing
in the hall. No one ever bothered with

Soutine from day to day, but he was asking
for it this time. The building smelled like rotting flesh.
The landlord pounded on the door. "You bastard!"

"*Go away!*" "Enough, Soutine. Unless
you haul that garbage from the building
I will have *you* hauled away." This fresh

affront made Chaïm throw down the brush. "You're killing
me! I told you fifty times—*I paint!*
This is my studio." The landlord was unwilling

to put up with it, and a complaint
was filed. The gendarmes were the next to knock.
"Soutine, you have to let them in." This faint,

exhausted plea from Paulette hit him like a rock.
He stopped his painting, calmly turned around,
unlocked the door, and opened it. The shock

was registered succinctly when the gendarme found
the carcass hanging in a buzz of flies.
"Explain, monsieur." The captain looked around

as Soutine plied him with apologies
and Paulette fumbled with the swatting broom.
He saw the three completed pictures. "These

are marvelous," he mumbled, and the room
depressurized. The sympathetic officer
allowed the tired painter to assume

the mantle of an artist in the aperture
of his protected space. No law applied.
"I agree you should continue here, monsieur,

but how securely have you got this tied?"
He checked the knots and nodded in approval.
"Are you familiar with formaldehyde?"

He suggested opening a window. The removal
of the body was postponed until the weekend,
giving Soutine three more days. In all

that time, Paulette would later swear, her friend
remained awake and working. They hardly spoke.
Soutine, his shoulders hunched, would lean against

a chair and load a brush and lunge. He broke
a dozen brushes in a day. Three times
he tried to eat—but eating made him choke.

Paulette would pull the bowl away. "Oh, Chaïm,
you need to stop." "I'll finish when
it falls apart." It fell. And from the slime

his hanging carcass series rose to 10,
each painting fully spread with crucified
and falling cattle, seething gristle end-

to-end. On Saturday, the thing would slide
across the floor and down the stairs and out,
a golem slab extinguished in a tide

of passion, fallen in a savage bout
of extra rounds. Soutine himself collapsed.
Zborowski paid to sanitize the rout

and crossed the landlord's palm. Paulette, perhaps
intuiting an impact on the painter's
ulcer, diagnosed exhaustion as a relapse—

she'd seen him through the throes of stomach pain.
Her premonition, her experience,
and her devotion would serve him well again.

F RA ANGELICO AT THE MET

2 December 2005

The careful, golden light
holds them all – the wounded

supplicant, leg crooked and
bandaged foot, the rotund
cleric who drops a coin

in an open palm, the
calm virgin, and the child
on her lap, reaching out

to the world – the solid
flesh, round limbs and faces,
peaceful eyes. What burdens

there are – the crucified
God, somehow in repose,
or the crippled beggar

balanced on his crutch – are
made beautiful, an all-
too-human transgression,

a strange kindness, so that
the torment of the sick,
of the tortured martyrs,

their headless bodies that
once were bathed in pain, and

are now covered with the
light of grace, are simply

a matter of course, bright
red spatters of blood an

inevitable turn
of events, like the folds
of the red and green robes

of witnesses and of
victims alike. Rilke

must have been thinking of
him when he asked, whom can
we ever turn to in

our need – the light, at last,
a mystery to the
lost and to the redeemed.

WITH FRED CARUSO, STANDING IN FRONT OF PIERRE BONNARD'S *CORNER OF THE DININGROOM AT LE CANNET*

"The Late Interiors," Metropolitan Museum of Art,
New York City, 27 March 2009

Nothing much ever happens, yet there
is a comfort in simply living
among the objects of the day — bowls
of fruit, a vase of flowers on a
red tablecloth holding light coming
from a window outside of the frame.

Her face is turned sideways above her
bright yellow shawl as she looks for what
she has meant to take with her, leaving
the room — or is she, in a backward
glance at the urn on the mantelpiece,
admiring her arrangements of things?

Fred and I stand talking, the painting
of the dining room behind him, and
I think about Bonnard's soft tones, then
about Fred's portrayals in their hot
colors, his people — young and full with
desire, and smiling at the viewer.

In Bonnard's picture we slowly come
to notice a faint longing in the
day itself — the woman's dissolving
thought, what she wants still remaining, like
the scene before us, which is not quite
real but true enough for the moment.

Erotica

THE FIG

My lover fills all things with love's perfume,
but I, distracted, lose the scent in names:
words without sense, vacant experience.

This flower becomes no more than *white rose*,
the desert: *wasteland*, myself: *labyrinth*.
On the table sits a plate of dried fruit;

I reach for it and hold in my right hand
a fig: dull flesh, sad as a withered breast.
Had no one shown me, told me: *Take and eat,*

I should never have tasted its sweetness.
Between my fingers I split the fig's skin
and find in it a galaxy of seeds

glistening, as if wet, in the sunlight.
The torn skin is delicately petalled
like the tender gate to my lover's womb.

BIOLOGICAL GALAXIES

Consider our bodies, precise systems
of tubes and glands,
the synaptic hurdle jumping
of sensation, pain reception's
Morse code, how bile duct and liver
are a little factory of workers.

Your every cell is a galaxy,
with its own ellipses and orbits,
each organelle a satellite circling,
nuclei like miniature suns
lighting up your insides.
You carry oceans within,
comprised of water as you are,
your pulse the universe's rhythm,
that interaction of gases
and matter and heat.

So it's no mistake when I tell you
your movements are tidal,
or that I want you close
because gravity is like that.

THE STARS

What can I say about your mouth
That has not already been said
About the stars, how in their
Regular rotations they speak
About something greater then themselves,
Something unseen and mysterious.

And if I believe
In an interior landscape,
I believe you are full of stars.
Each star a galaxy
Invisibly connected and alive.

If I believe in the unseen
It is because of you
And the memory of your kisses.

A thousand reasons
May shout, proclaiming
The truth of the visible,

But I believe in your kiss.

BECAUSE I DO NOT LOVE YOU

I can love you calmly
like the dogwood turns
its leaf buds and cream
petals to the April light
and softly they stir the air.

I can love you
because I can look away

And watch through a window
listening to the silent voices
singing in high-pitched keys,
the whistles of dogs, the stretching
trees and rushing bats.

I can look away
and not make you the sun

As love can make a sun of the moon
and stars of dark eyes—
how lost and confusing the cosmic map
when constellations
must be traced with held hands.

I do not make you the sun
and can see you

Puttering about the house
arranging your own natural
order to your things,
see the sweet surprise
when you lift your eyes to me.
I can see you,
can love you calmly.

Nathan Swartzendruber

2009 Opaque Projectionist

SPECIFIC GRAVITY

He unzipped her dress with the expression
of a dog unused to being outdoors in the rain.
She didn't see. It was night, the city twilight
that's best explained by planes turning above
the grid, resolving the cloud of white noise
rising to the sky by condensing it to contrails.
They ride the light, drafting higher
from street row to street, their weight
pressing down the air like ships contain
the sea: with wings. Keeping teak tables
from floating off patios, them both from
bobbing against the balcony french doors
when he slides the straps of the summer
slender dress off her shoulders. How
he wished he could see her from further
away. How he wished he could see them
both when he turned her by the shoulders
to kiss her mouth, a full revolution away.

GREEN

> *Verde, que te quiero verde.*
> *Garcia Lorca*

> *No matter what you do,*
> *at last you will be overwhelmed,*
> *the distance will be broken,*

> *the music will confound you.*
> *Theodore Weiss*

I want to be overwhelmed, broken,
confounded once again
by that young summer,
when we chased horses in the pasture
and bridled them into submission,
when we lay soft and tangled against
each other in the hot afternoon hay.

Deep within the heat
of that summer I knew
that all I knew
of green belonged to you.

THE RED HANDKERCHIEF

I.

The hustler leans against the hotel,
muddy eyes fixed on space,
dreaming about his single lucky star
impaled on its spire,
about a bird with carmine wings to carry him off
beyond the stain of his horizon.

A red handkerchief hangs out his pocket,
it is the flag of his desire:
a whole hand sliding into him
and clenching,
his voice lost inside a pillow.

The young ones strut back and forth
beneath the awning, its bare aluminum frame
faded green. Who is green?
Where is a man with thick arms
to take him in, the single customer he wants,
the dead explosions
that were once his life to him?

II.

Sometimes I see you standing by the fruit-market
or on the island
sparse with old men on benches,
gliding back and forth for a whisper, a call.

I see a red curtain flapping out a window,
imagine it's yours:
your tiny room with its cracked walls and armchair,
a pewter bowl holding a single, bruised pear.

Here's the bed where you sigh for them,
legs hiked around their shoulders,
here are the bills that keep rustling on the nightstand,
the clank of buckles,
trousers piled on the floor.

If I looked at you hard,
would you look back, or wrinkle and say
nothing, *not good enough*,
the choice yours to say no?

III.
You let the wind dare to stroke you
before the light
fails,
before the night wheeling the sky
with stars and dogs
who dance the tango in their minds.
You let the wind
sweetly finger
your scalp, the naked arms,
the handkerchief now spread over
your crotch,
a handkerchief almost orange,
the color of blood,
a red handkerchief that keeps flapping
your dry loins.

IV.
We should be allies sweetly dancing
out the doors of this hotel,
past the doorman inside his uniform,
under the awning, watch the clouds blowing past.

We should be touching scores of lights off
in our wake, push the dark back inside us,
sailing handkerchiefs, the rose between our teeth,
fling them off into the night.

When I look at you I wonder
if I'm flesh or something greater.
I haven't fought for my life
or desire, haven't felt the fist rising
through my bowels, cried in anger or victory,
my flesh broken and singing.

I want to step from beneath this awning,
into the wind, the flaring sun,
want those clouds to mean
hope instead of loss.

THE TAO OF LONGING

I am vexed with the most useless desires.
I want the smell of tallow in your hair
the ridges in the nails of your toes
the vein that wanders down your thigh
and the wheat in your voice.
I want the lick of salt
that hurries down your neck.
I want the air that you expel
that reels with the damp of your lungs
and the delirium of carbon dioxide.
And I want the moon, in its nest of clouds.
And the snap of acorns,
falling, falling in the night.

esoterica

ΝΕΜΕΑ

Through sunlit woods the Master stalked his prey,
marking where it had left its fearful trace.
Alone, a roar has signaled their embrace,
and all is still. The sun sinks with the day.
Past fields and thickets, hurrying away
towards Tiryns, scared, a shepherd slows his pace
to turn. In fear his eyes bulge from his face,
beholding through the trees the beast at bay.
He screams. He sees beneath a sky of blood
with open jaws the Terror of the Wood
shaking its mane and grinning for the feast.
It is the shadow dusk has magnified
of Hercules draped in the fearful hide,
a monstrous hero, mingling man and beast.

TREATISES IN THE GROUND

for Victoria Nelson

I left my house. I was nine years old,
where Seven Locks Road meets Tuckerman Lane;
I left my house. I was nine years old.
      I headed down the path.
My knapsack filled with kryptonite
and a dogeared copy of *Sein und Zeit*,
the cabbage trees were green and white
      and sparkled with God's wrath.

I came to the house of Sally O'Neill,
where the rain falls hot on Ravensbane;
I came to the house of Sally O'Neill
      and knocked upon her door.
It opened wide. She said Come in.
You can put your knapsack there by the fin
of the dead sea-monster in yon bin
      of boiling blood and gore.

She was ten years old with coal-black hair,
where Seven Locks Road meets Tuckerman Lane;
she was ten years old with coal-black hair
      and ivory-colored skin.
She looked a sight in her dress so formal.
Like Wednesday Addams but not as normal.
Tell mortals nothing and the worm tell
      that you are his kin.

Let us go down to the creek she said,
where the rain falls hot on Ravensbane;
Let us go down to the creek she said.
          Her hands described an arc.
I'll change my shoes and darn my socks.
We'll look for pebbles and stumbling-blocks
and the salamanders under the rocks
          so venomous and so dark.

She took a jar from the mantlepiece,
where Seven Locks Road meets Tuckerman Lane.
She took a jar from the mantlepiece
          all cluttered with gnarly things
like horseshoe crabs and oyster beds,
divining rods and shrunken heads
with bloodshot eyes and tangled dreads
          and a stone for augurings.

I picked up the stone and said What's this?
where the rain falls hot on Ravensbane.
I picked up the stone and said What's this?
          O won't you please expand?
It's a seer stone that my father found
while looking for treatises in the ground.
And, moving closer, without a sound
          she plucked it from my hand

and held it up to her violet eyes,
where Seven Locks Road meets Tuckerman Lane.
And held it up to her violet eyes
          and this is what she said:
I'm Sally O'Neill and I can see things
inside this stone for augurings:
the broken rungs and ancient springs,
          the thresholds of the dead.

I'm Sally O'Neill and I can see things,
where the rain falls hot on Ravensbane.
I'm Sally O'Neill and I can see things.
        She put the stone in a hat.
With hardly any breathing-space,
she put the hat around her face
to seek the serpent's hiding-place
        within this habitat.

And what do you see in the stone? said I,
where Seven Locks Road meets Tuckerman Lane;
And what do you see in the stone? said I
        with fearful voice so low.
Why do you tremble, my little man?
It is not wicked thus to scan
the flat, antediluvian
        divining-stone to know

the creek sleeps over the thick black mud,
where the rain falls hot on Ravensbane.
The creek sleeps over the thick black mud
        where lurks the slimy eel,
the snapping turtle and the frog,
the pumpkin and the polliwog,
the puppets made of straw and fog,
        and by a wagon-wheel

not two yards from the barn's hex sign,
where Seven Locks Road meets Tuckerman Lane;
not two yards from the barn's hex sign,
        you waspy little prig,
there's a willow tree with blood that drips
and under that tree above the crypts
a coffer of sacred manuscripts.
        We'll find it if we dig.

So we took a shovel and an old pick-axe,
where the rain falls hot on Ravensbane;
so we took a shovel and an old pick-axe
        out to the sunken field.
We dug and dug. The moon rose high.
Behold the glimmer in her eye
when the pick-axe hit the scoriae
        and they began to yield.

I'm Sally O'Neill and look what I've found,
where Seven Locks Road meets Tuckerman Lane:
a coffer of treatises in the ground.
        We'll take it home right now
and put it next to the almanac,
(Poimandres the salamander stashed in back)
and all the stars in the zodiac
        will glitter on my brow.

She walked beside me in the dark,
where the rain falls hot on Ravensbane;
she walked beside me in the dark
        and we could hardly see.
Then, parting from me in the night,
she handed me the coffer, quite
as if somehow she knew by right
        the scrolls belonged to me.

I scan those texts by the light of the moon,
where Seven Locks Road meets Tuckerman Lane;
I scan those texts by the light of the moon,
        bent over every page.
By the light of the moon by the light of the sun
I search each word. I've just begun.
My studying will not be done
        till I am gray with age.

Richard Darabaner

2012 Plaint

RECRIMINATION:
A SONG OF GENERATIONS

You rend me from the only days
In which the tender thread to heaven
I was to weave
In the fabric of forgottenness was lost.

Gentleness, with your old song of them
A little longer

As if the galled sundering
Did not resound those days yours
As I shall recite them mine hereafter

As if the days
Would be unforgotten
For me alone

So many of your reasons ensnare
My entrail-blue fish
Folded in the whitening mass.

It was your shallows
The shoal was reefed on
It was your darkening gates
Kept me from speaking
The one small way none of you knew He was listening.

Note:
The lost secret of the species of fish whose special quality was to be used to make the blue thread of the prayer shawl is here compared to the obscuring of the special duty for which each person was created.

THE SIMPLE WORLD

I boarded an ancient gringo school bus
reborn to carry people, chickens, and pigs,
taking on a mountain curve at higher speed

than a red Camaro floors the Interstate.
The sacred Virgin of Guadalupe prayed
over her playmate sister. Both dangled

from silver chains below the rearview mirror.
On the windshield, yellow script proclaimed, *Jesús,
mi salvador.* The driver wore dark glasses.

I maneuvered past families sharing child-sized
two-seaters, kids on parents' laps,
fathers' legs in the aisles, and found space

beside a boy who leaned against the window.
On his knees, he held a mottled rooster.
Its beak and feet were tied with sewing thread.

The bus lurched forward and soon rocked to and fro,
snaking through mountains stippled purple and green,
halting when the *ayudante* banged the roof

or a passenger whistled, crying, *Baja aquí!*
The boy fell asleep beside me, eyelids fluttering.
Through his nose, he whistled a dream song.

Dust swirled a halo around his face.
I wanted to dab the sweat that beaded
his terra cotta lips, to touch an open shirt snap

that rose and fell with every breath. Seeing me
watch his master, the captive rooster blinked. I'm thirsty,
its eye implored when I sipped from my canteen.

I stared out the window, above the rooster's crown
at the cinematic stills that shift the world:
a sable horse munching grass. White church

no bigger than a hut, weathervane
piercing a cloud. Children playing barefoot
among sheep. I wanted all the simple world

for mine. The boy woke and smiled drowsily,
his forehead damp, his beautiful lips chapped.
I offered my canteen. He reached

and grabbed my breast, then stole his hand away—
less than a minute could have passed.
The rooster shut its eye and seemed to dream.

At the front of the bus, I glanced down
at my breast. It burned though I was innocent.

THE COPPER SCROLL

for Gustaf Sobin

As fire lies in wood
& wine lies in the vine

as night lies in the mountain
or the way the river lies in the ice

the crater in the desert,
empty shells in a reef

where glittering fish
repose in the dark.

As repose itself hides
in geese rising through

an Arctic iridescence.
As heat hides in limbs,

kisses in the lips, fate
in delirious plans

for a secret wedding, & the
dress lies in the needle & thread,

& in the satin radiance
from the beginning,

opening like a banner of light
over violet buds, or a single

red leafed tree in the wet,
or feathers in the wing,

or an horizon that goes
unbroken in the fog, like

a stone tree in a stone forest
sunk under the sea like

a sum under a list of numbers . . .
Be patient in the earth, jewel.

Perfections afar, draw near.
The full moon lies hidden in

a wisp dipped in clouds.
Our true lives lie hidden

like the inventory of the temple
(in anticipation of its destruction)

in 64 places around the world,
in clay pots, tureens, sacks

riches hidden like the peak
of the fire in the flue

or air in an ice floe
or, in a wall, a gold box

the weight of a small animal.
The copper scroll lies

pried from clay, X-rayed,
gripped by scholars.

The nooks it names
have all been scoured.

No trove, no ghost of a trove.
But the scraps of script do not lie.

Emptiness, be our wealth,
a truth to be treasured, like

a ruby in a spray of garnets
or a memorial at dawn,

like 10 talents hidden in a canal
or, under large paving stones,

6 silver bars. In the stream
west of Kohlit, bowls, tubes,

libation vessels, 609 in all.
East of the esplanade

(as dreams lie within waking,
as light lies in the turns of the earth)

in pools, courtyards & caves —
the nill, the naught, the neither . . .

& in the hills, to the north,
under a tamarisk tree,

& in the waterfall at the mouth
of the gorge of Bet Tamar . . .

I R C A M

Tonight we are experiencing acoustical weather.
"one must learn to hear silence"
apparently begins with a long hum,
not a hunt for melody but the structure
of chance, the cello recycled to echo
its shadowy self, elongated, flattened,
as we have come to suppose the sound
of space, which is never empty, has resonance
without walls, resources in black holes
round the still hall, a holy cultic choir
where no one has a cold, rubs his girl's arm,
where hard pews favor a mechanical aesthetic,
the technique assuming each an ascetic,
where experts more than amateurs preside.
Play it again, Sam.

READING THE GEORGICS

Words seem to fade into the page,
just as trees outside the ice-streaked
window are gathered into the darkening sky.

Per duodena regit mundi sol aureus astra,
The golden sun rules all twelve constellations . . .

. . . under which sign to plant yellow barley
after clearing wild pulse, slender vetch,
reedy lupine stalks.

Catalogued as if they were
epic heroes: grains, winds, birds.
Scylla flees her father hawk on little wings.

Which vines grow best in local soils. Anthrax,
ruin of fields and flocks. Aristaeus transfixed
by the resounding rivers of Cyrene's cave.

Laboresque lunae, moon's labors.
Iustissima terra, Earth most proportionate.

Stasis and reduction. Inert trees
sapless, skeletonized, snow- shrouded.

Strokes of green
arise from unbound soil,
gradually become legible.

MEDITATIONS

Salt is good. Fire is tribulation & salt is God's word.
Every man shall be *salted with fire*; every sacrifice
shall be seasoned with salt. But if salt loses its savor,
how will it be salted? Keep the salt in yourself. And the salt is
a fire.
   An inwardness of fire soothes though *the gliding fires*
of heaven do live. Hemispherical. Transformative.
Waters seethe with flame. Fear of baptism is fear of fire.
In a fantasy, the Holy feed off sublime light; bite
their Pentecostal tongues lolling with glossolalia. Paint
bubbles, peels, gasses before ever liquefying.
Icons tossed on a bonfire are twice-scorched: by the gross flames
that consume the wood like kindling & by the glassy
ellipse of light each icon inwardly stokes with splinters of
Paradise.

    I am your Consummator & I strive
after Images. The Lord of Fire outlaws all extinguishers.
At the troughs of sublime light, the Holy feed, porcine &
glazed with honey. All the tastier for the feast of the
Holy Spirit, who hungers. And craves salted flesh. The fires
of devotion tenderize our earthy souls, musked as truffles,
hidden from the light in a soil where they cohere. Into
a tuber. A mind. An egg.

     Beatitude is a spice.
A flavor of spiritual heat. Lest we forget. Blessèd
Holy One retreating into the collapsing, receding
Radiation of light.

Our God is mobile, increasing
where once he remained hidden. His increase balloons into
pleroma, a life as transcendent gas. Dangerous &
flammable. Would you worry yourself with questions of his
weakness, even as his shape surprises you as a thing
unknowable? It is amazing that a man does not
die when uttering the call to prayer. In the cosmos
that shapes God's feelings, you are a novice. Angels,
trailing scents of anise & dill, intervene in the sphere of fire
cushioning God's otherworldly immanence. Fire beings
guarding the Throne, hideous & hybrid: human, bovine,
leonine, aquiline. Unnatural, composite.
Immobile in that they expand from God's emanating
circumference but never invent themselves apart from it.
Cherubim & Seraphim are the bursts of sudden weather
in the atmosphere of God.

Knowledge is fire, not symbolic.
Igneous fluids drain from the dragon sinus of God
into a parched throat, gruff with blistered vocables, red as
a blazing carbuncle. Gunpowder peppers the chimney
corrosive vitriol & oil of fires sheen. Creosote,
resin, turpentine. Fire is the phenomenon that has
most preoccupied chemists, seeking the salt, the sulphur,
the mercury that allow it to slide through time. Like a
living creature, fire feeds itself. Hard to light; difficult
to put out. This is God. The universal empire of
fire.

Sown light in the cobalt blue flame of the sky. Gas
jet of it refined in the scattering. An unruly
providence dangles downward through the radiant cones of
burning salt, burning mercury. It lolls with angelic

authorities, a vague spaciousness, a material
foam. Flecked with God-stuff.

Sown light in the cobalt blue flame of
the sky. Who strewed it? Who treated magnetic plasma as
bones, as a skeleton? Lavished it with flesh, with a breath?
Simple pulsed fume of atmosphere. Rotating Ptolemaic
dome of catastrophe-ash we live in, remotely. In
the outside, an emanator, regressing. Energy
as of a nylon bunched up then stretched in the thinnest
kinetics.

Sown light in the cobalt blue. In the jet flame
of the sky. An Abrahamic prophet is a syllable
spiller. His speech is closer to God than even a
sanctioned idea. The Lord reposes in the nest of
his dentition. As he spits out stars. As he pastes himself
with privations. Fasts. As he ignores the sacrifices.
Gnawing on his tongue instead.

Sown light. I would not tell you
what to do with it. No I would not tell you what to do
with it. Would not.

Nearby, gel puddles. The One who sees God
starts fire, burns a pillar with hellish signs, looks on an
aniconic corpus blurred with tongues, with coals. Weeping wastes
the better part of vision. Rather pray. Look where the in-
most in you pools. The perplexing headdress of the Lord looks
back from the curdling mercury of the soul, a feast. But
who having seen this Image wouldn't rather starve? Wouldn't
rather devour flame, in roaring gulps. Sentience encinders
the brush of thought, of patience, of prayer; settles in a lace
of smoke, drifted up from a stick of incense, an ash of worry.

Silence aspirates, a lung, an aether. Books resemble
flames, huffing oxygen, grotesque. One taper burns, a sabbath.
A staretz said: if you strive to enter the inner cell
of your soul, there you will discover the cell of heaven.
Inwardness & paradise: in each case, wordless. Ever
a shapeliness. A lozenge of honey soothed along the ribs
of the palate, shaped as if by vibration or a womb
into a sliver of glass—: a golden glucose. There is
no union with the Lord. The union is within, beyond
the Godhead. Lips pulsate with prayer, its breath an aura.

THE SORROWS OF EROS

I

Eros would gather up the golden sheaves
Strewn on the path that rumination leaves
In ruins mouldering till the end of time.

This was a path where solitude was known
To every singularity as its own;
The many were as one alone in this.

He was a being; others were the same;
So much by way of kinship he could claim,
Kinship consisting here in otherness.

Among so many beings, being shone,
Held for a moment, hovered, then was gone:
Nothing for long could house or hold it in.

The glimmering world, the world beyond our ken,
That was a way to formulate it then,
Hallowed and hollowed out of emptiness.

Therefore the sages held it up to scorn,
Deeming it better not to have been born,
Since every form informed futility.

Life lives our life, the ancient poet said,
And ruthlessly each useless skin is shed:
The serpent only writhes to writhe again.

Such were the ruminations that were torn
From Eros early on a summer morn
Before the corn grown green against the sky.

II

Silence and solitude, oppressive pain
Of repetition with its old refrain,
In runes are graven on the human heart.

In runic letters not to be devised,
Inscrutable inscriptions are incised:
We come upon them sometimes in the dark.

The humus of the human, thick and deep,
Pulls heavily upon us as we sleep.
It covers us and closes up our eyes.

III

He sought the sources of the ancient springs,
The luminous and liquid solacings
That language proffers us against the void.

What if those glints upon the shifting stream,
Imputing depth to every common dream,
Were fatuous fires – a play of surfaces?

Or as the last philosopher had said,
What if those depths to which we thought they led
Revealed at last that nothing was concealed?

Would prosody protect them from the truth?
Romanticism was the dream of youth
Who thought that prosody protected them.

IV

Negative Capability . . . To cede
The initiative to words – a modest creed
The Enlightenment and skepticism spawned.

Syntax was certainty: to fathom sound
Until the plangency of sense was found
And luminescence glowed on simple speech.

How strange that in an instantaneous stroke
Uncanny combinations could evoke
The icy floes or melt the tears of things.

Speaker and spoken to were then undone:
Nobody knew, not ever, no, not one,
Whence it arose, that flowering into song.

Nobody ever knew the simplest thing.
Doubt that had flourished, withered, flourishing
Suspicion spun itself into a web.

What if the whole procedure were a slick
Conjuring trick of sophist rhetoric,
A sleight of hand beguiling and beguiled?

Syntax was certainty – and what it mined
Painstakingly, in faith, could be refined:
The craft was sure, however crude the ore.

V

In his perambulations round the lake
He sought contingency, both for the sake
Of what it was and what it might reveal.

Experience, thus, was to be cherished for
Itself and as a kind of metaphor
For what it pointed to but could not reach.

He led a life of allegory then,
Winged on the words that rose up through his pen,
Where what had been abstract was made concrete.

Sometimes a Great Blue Heron would appear,
Angling its elegance in morning air,
Always when one was least expecting it;

Or soaring oriole uplifted high,
Bright blotch of yellow blazoning the sky,
Gathered within the topmost branches' green.

Swans in their silence, simple and complex,
Beauty's enigma curved on slender necks,
Circled the surface, mirrored in the deep.

At other times desire found no surcease:
Nothing but common terns and hissing geese,
Or crows caw-cawing as in mockery.

Perpetual cardinals and painted jays,
Plumed though in glory, palled upon his gaze,
Familiarity disfiguring them.

Boredom, depression, stasis, ennui,
Modernity's prosaic progeny,
Flaunted their dismal feathers in disdain.

Shadows lengthened; it was growing late –
Which meant one had to be compassionate,
And bear the burden of the mystery.

And evening echoed the consoling dove,
Calling to mind Francesca's gentle love
And Mallarmé's great *tombeau* on Verlaine.

VI

The saddest quandary was how to live
Without the encumbrance of a narrative,
Complacent fiction or consoling lie.

Incessantly one sought the hidden laws
That secretly determined what one was,
As if one's fate were written in the stars.

And like a destiny the poem lay
Buried beneath the language, far away,
But waiting in its truth to be revealed.

One knew, of course, that nothing was the same
And never could be traced to whence it came
Through tangled passageways of origin.

One knew that being, being various,
Was arbitrary and fortuitous
In what it manifested or erased.

And in that knowledge one had grown resigned
To the abysses of a darkened mind
That tossed and plummeted in its own space.

(What proverb, precept or apt apothegm
Allayed such moments, being wrought from them?
Not to inflict on others one's own pain.)

Yet still one hungered for the Absolute,
Subordinating as if destitute
The green of summer, gold of autumn days.

And waiting for the waters to arise
Upon encrusted-thick velleities,
One spent one's time embellishing the myth:

Beauty is that which fills us with despair,
Authenticating by its presence there
The Orphic explanation of the earth.

The echoes still resounded, but the tale
From long-time telling had grown flat and stale,
Heavily weighted with ambivalence.

The ghosts of longing lingered on the shore.
– What if one didn't need them anymore?
Would they be dissipated in the mist?

Or, broken upon the rocks, bleeding and torn,
Naked as on the day that one was born,
Was one to be dismembered with the rest?

No one could say; no murmur from the Muse:
There seemed no point in probing for her views,
Which were, one knew, at variance from one's own.

Where could one go and what was there to find?
Nothing, perhaps, and nowhere; never mind:
In any case, at last one was alone.

A LOOK AT THE DOOR WITH THE HINGES OFF

1

In white suits, on a white-washed terrace, Pound and Fenol-
losa sat at a white painted wrought iron table with a glass top,
drinking milky white drinks, ouzu perhaps or a mixture of milk
and water. At that time, Fenollosa had grown a rather large
black moustache which stood out against the whiteness of the
scene like one of his inimitable Chinese characters.

2

In white suits, pagination permitted, the terrace washed in
white paint, a light rain had fallen, which now the heat of the
sun, pulsating behind the clouds, changed to steam. Ouzu
was brought out by the waitress, a young girl with very white
skin whose dark eyes hung in the white space of the scene
like two dots in the negative of a photograph taken through a
telescope trained on Sirius and Canis.

3

In control of the whites, Franz Kline claimed he was not a
calligrapher, painting the white portions of his later canvases
with as much concern as he showed for the blacks. Canis and
Fenollosa would have gotten along well together.

4

We have a problem with white. It is the grace of saying it.
Something we like—a flash of color, an absolute aimlessness
to our intensity—the world will suffer less.

5

At every point a node of energy clung to the white wool of her
dress. It was all very sexy.

6

The grand themes demand a certain silence, a sense of qui-
etude which precludes pompous utterance. Here, my dearest,
the ubiquity of the world in clean white sheets.

ANGELOLOGY

The angel is expanding at the interceded light.
Abraham flattered our time with monologue; intrepid
holoplast of God spoke back. Three visitors arrived at
the afternoon's hot-point. Wordless. Placid? A meal was set.
Fervently. Things are innumerable prolongations of
divine being. Star-sockets fizzle over generations
of the circumcised. Inwardness of fire soothes the burning
blade. Did Abraham reckon the life beyond life? Or did he
invent it? Since his contract with starlight, we live for
increasing an exemplification of the angel's
life, potential in the cycled horizon of time in
our chest-cavity, gained by an auto-intellection—:
prayer, interiority. We inherit Abraham's
power of seeing, obliquely. As a human tendency.
The angel is an emotion. He arrives out of
profound intuition. Not a higher but an inner order.

The terrain of the afterworld is your imagination
of it, which is to say an automatic impression
of nonequilibrium, of an unstable system.
Time is not what we perceive—some relativity—but
we are what time perceives through. Like spectacles. Irises.
Think of angels then as magnifiers. Binoculars
for the birdwatcher, Time. Like matter, Chronos is a self-
organizing maker of dissipative structures.
How can the Heavenly City from which these messengers
emanate be otherwise? The system of the universe
is an unstable empire, migrating inwards. Angels
activate the flux.

Perplexed by motionless time, outside
what is intelligible, they range inward in the push
of known time, in motion there. They are themselves bodies
wholly intelligent. The material elements
of the universe pass from one angelic body to
another, so that the creation is but a single
body. The intelligible is not eternal. St
Basil wrote: As the beginning of a road is not yet
the road, & the beginning of a house is not yet a
house, so the beginning of time is not yet time, not even
the smallest part of it. Creation—created time—is
instantaneous. Angels, arrayed in cyclic motion,
by function look inward toward God, never seeing beyond.
Abraham swelters on Mamre. The three angels cool on
paradisaical ice their eyes radiate, seeing ХΡС
several thousand years hence. Time jerks, a buckle on a bull-
whip, languorously snapped.
                              The perfection of these angels
is Abraham's perfection. Seeing him they see heaven
uncreated; through him they bear perfect witness to time
unclotted at last. Abraham sets the meal, hurries jars
of water to his visitors. Sarah is rewarded
with Isaac, promised. Her laugh is prophetic seal. Goats &
sheep ruminate in moonless afternoon. Abraham con-
celebrates with invisible fires invisibly winged.

POEM ABOUT TIME WITH LIONS

– from a recipe by Mindy Brown

After the great clock of day winds down, all cages
spring open, their guards taken suddenly by sleep;
all pens, corrals, sheepfolds fall away.
The lions of darkness roam the elementary schools,
loaf on the steps of temples, yawn at themselves in the mirrors
of storefronts, ponder the still fountains of malls.
They weep into small pots where later, rare salts appear
like tea leaves spelling fortunes.

Past midnight, the lions begin to smolder, their temperatures
rising past boiling to the point where gold will melt.
Sagging at first, then softening, they begin to
flow, whole Africas of them, down
the small town's streets, through busy intersections
in the suburbs, through the pink bedrooms of cheerleaders
into the back alleys of our bodies: floods of lions,
mudslides of lions, our bellies, faces, groins
awash with melted lions.

We rub their oils and musks all over us, gild our bodies
with their wild gold, drench our beds in the butter
of their softness, until they gather themselves back together.
Mane, claw, tooth reappear like the Cheshire Cat's
lost grin; they snarl at our fleeing house cats,
snap the legs off our yapping lap dogs, gobble our lives,

even the bone-hard knots of them—jail terms, sicknesses, sins—
multiplying one hundred times every injury we receive,
adding to our woes their bleak tonnages of sorrow.

Then, licking their bloody fur, they apologize for nothing.
When even Jesus passes in our dreams, smiling,
palms up, on his way to some pleasant work in Cana,
they remain unmoved, gorged in an alien sleep.

S C R I B E

You enter the city with harps and with flutes,
with drums and with baskets
of grapes and pomegranates.
You enter the city of blue ash and blue spruce,
that terraced city rumored of the spirit.

You come there as would a fire,
but neither you nor anything you touch is burned.
There is no sign upon you,
but there are signs upon the doorposts,
amulets of silver shaped like a hand
with letters upon the palm and fingers.

You wander into the little streets
unguarded by leopards or the statues of leopards,
where love is brought to you like an offering
stolen from the altar of a civic deity
who blesses the family with contentment.

You may say you have failed your calling,
that your riches and your debts have taken you this far
and will take you farther, you who have traded
upon yourself and upon the idols that you broke and reassembled.

You have written a history of renunciation
and a genealogy of indulgence,
mistaking pleasure for experience
and experience for wisdom.
You have raised your voice against the sufficiency of silence,
and answered by silence you were silenced,
but never with sufficient severity
and never without sufficient hope.

You have heeded the word of the outside god
and you have heeded the word of no god at all,
like a prophet turned archaeologist,
a scribe turned into a scribe.

ESCAPADE

after the folk tale

Every gingerbread man takes
the shadow shape of a featureless child and runs
as far as Eliza could go over the ice, as far as
Kozinsky could go through the woods of *The Painted Bird*
as far as Harriet Jacobs/Linda Brent
could go and call her children North to her
as far as the African names could run around Newark and
    New York
and the child of hot streets bear up under those long names
Shakkima, Al-Quan, Kahrriniyyah, Daeshaun, Gbasay,
    Zakiyyah
But the Fox is always coming up the path from below
the frame/ the page
with sharp teeth
with great scraggly belly,
and the Latin sun
broils the skin of memory,
makes a desert of the mind

The mind may be seeking pathways back
to water, island dreams of sheltering trees
but words, the indispensable baggage, are lost en route

and every child knows what happens to the gingerbread man,
    that brave cookie.

Coda:
But doesn't he get away, you ask.
Oh yes, he certainly gets away, and he becomes the child of
    those people
who made him
what he was, that cut-out.

LIKE DATES AND ALMONDS, PURPLE CLOTH & PEARLS

in memory of Robert Rethy

We entered by the middle gate
because the first gate frightened us
with the ox and the pit, the destruction and the fire.
We were old men and we were children
old men disguised as children
long ago and yesterday and the day after tomorrow.

We dreamed of it and spoke of it
dreamed that we spoke of it
spoke of it and wrote of it
upon parchments of deerskin.
With the meat we fed the orphans
and on the skins wrote the five books
and took the books to the city
where there were no teachers
and taught five children the five books
and six children the six orders
and told them: We shall return
but in the meantime let each of you
teach his book and his order to all the others.

It was like that and like nothing else
like nothing else in the city
and like nothing in that generation.
It was nothing like nostalgia
though it was said to be all nostalgia

like a word twisted into a ring
and like a ring lost in a deep pool
and like a ring found in the belly of a fish
that spoke so it might return to the sea.

It was built by the water so as to wait there.
The word came from across the water
the word flowed into other words
the water poured down and we stood there naked
looking out to a horizon that stretched across the world.
We wanted to go back and would have
had it not been for all the errors
in the memories and in the recording of the memories
and in the recording of the recording
in the city of cities across the water.

We wanted it to go on and it did go on
though it stopped and it turned and so turned up
elsewhere wherever between here and the river
that threw up stones for six days out of seven.
We could not rest though we longed for rest
we had returned though we did not think to return
we looked and we saw ourselves under the canopy of the horizon
and it was as we had been taught though we could no longer remember.

GEOGRAPHICA

CONCEPCION ISLAND

23 miles S/E of Cat Island
2.75 miles long

      2 miles across at its
      widest point

surrounded on its N/E and S sides
by reef
      watering place
      and sanctuary for birds

but otherwise
uninhabited

reminds me once again
that

      all worlds are
      small worlds

clustered
or standing alone

each with
      its own evolutionary
      history

atolls
of longing

the hardened shale
of volcanic anger

all worlds are
small worlds
variations
hedged by reefs
or mangroves
held

in the embrace
of imaginary
coordinates

LITTLE MISERY ISLAND

Some say you can walk across
From its larger kin. A gloss
I think on a darker fact:
All men are islands, compact

And irascible; low tide
Offers a way, an untried
Thoroughfare of murk and mud,
A convergence of lifeblood

To regenerate anew
A vision gone daft, askew,
And by most accounts diseased.
One would not be too displeased

To swim this channel of hurt,
A test of desperate effort,
Of metaphysical length
If one only had the strength.

GREAT MISERY ISLAND

Coiling white caps brace the grayness
The salt sea shrieks and shrieks again
Against the unchanging, anxious
Sky-vault, a lone and sorry man

On this island promontory;
Nearby the skeletons of ships
Sliding under, bones bleached—a jury
Of pernicious peers comes to grips

With its fate. Oak and maple groves
Offer light solace at dead end
Of each path above the curled coves,
Sanctuary from foe and friend.

This fractured heart with shaky hand,
Squeezing the soft wasted hour,
Searches out the limn of coastland
From lighthouse to sooty tower.

Then in darkness he descends down
Into his purgatory's void,
An unmodified man, a noun
Exposed to weather, unemployed

Until dawn, when he'll start to climb
Terrace after terrace. His pride
Peeled off: uncloaked, unreasoned crime
Bared to all. A lover shanghaied

By love. Beyond the breakwater
Of fate and sting of smaller hurts
Still his hopes persist; he totters
On and on, confounding the experts.

SAINT PAUL'S ROCKS

In the North Atlantic

The booby nests in salt-enameled slag.
Through fossiled ribs it breathes, a weathered gland.
The tern lays eggs on seaweed in the sand,
where Grapsus crabs in hiding wait to drag
a flying fish the male left for its mate
before our party scared her from the beach.
I've seen these crabs drag hatchlings to the breach—
they dart like lightning under twice their weight.
As for the other fauna, there are flies
and spiders and a kind of tick that might
be carried by the terns. There's not one tree.
There's little poetry for all the light
on this reluctant strand, for all the eyes
of timid birds that I have yet to see.

THE NIGHT FERRY

A starless night
enfolds the open harbor;
    the wind plays
its song with fir and cedar.

Out in the fog
a whistle sounds three times;
    beyond the dock
a slow murmur draws nearer.

Suddenly lights
give shape to a shimmering ship
    and snowflakes dissolve
into ripples of endless water.

The night ferry comes;
it stops to take me aboard
    where I can sleep
and journey a little farther.

NORTHERING

I am going
upstairs
by the ship ladder.
I will assemble
a bowl
of pears.
From a standing
dead forest.
From pecan
shells. Small views
of what's doing
in snow.
The planks
are milled. And me.
Hey season's folly.
Hey folly. Hey.

ALL SAINTS DAY

As we go north
the fire comes
together in little
petals of woe.

Where to go
in this general
conflagration?

Here we are
on this boulevard
bordered on both
sides by sand,

the exoskeletons
of the glittering
dead make a festival
in the moonlight.

But the muscles
intervene, protest
the encounter
with flame,

and harden,
crisp, sparkle,
and fall apart.

The north
enlarges, which is
to say, it goes
on forever.

PURE LUCK

When the whole busload of tourists from Germany
started to videotape me from outside the Spanish bar,
crowding against the windows on the hottest day
so far that summer in Seville, I didn't notice at first, inside
and immersed in dancing flamenco with a tuna –
a *strolling student band* – and my Mexican companion
making fun of the tuna we'd just eaten: *ensaladilla russa*,
Russian salad, a mix of tuna, egg and lots of mayonnaise, served
in all Spain's tapas bars, which ought to make it more Spanish
than Russian by now, and we'd already had enough of it,
of *tortilla española* and even of the strawberry popsicles
that kept saving us from that southern sun, so we felt lucky
when, later, we traveled back to France and ate each vegetable
in sight, though for all that we'd been happy with our time
in Andalucía, dancing in bars, keeping company with gypsies,
everything except those tourists pressing on the panes,
recording what they thought was a typical Spanish girl
doing typically Spanish things, not knowing my American
life and Russian Jewish roots as they tried to capture
me and so, a whole culture – an uneasy convergence
with the past: my grandmother lucky, if you can call it that, to survive,
the only one from her family, and my grandfather the only one
from his, though their stories are as much about the Tsar's army.
Well, what legacy is left to us in the end?
De puro churro, my companion quipped, *Pure luck*
when, hungry for something more as we fled the bar, we found
a *churros* stand and placed our orders just before it closed,

not caring the deep-fried pastries tasted of oil and batter both, just
grateful for the chocolate we dipped the churros into: a Spanish
tradition, that thick chocolate a dark lake you'd be glad
to sink into if you were lucky enough to also be saved.

WALKING RAMPART STREET

Degas the perfect *gentilhomme*
at home in Montparnasse

and Creole New Orleans
anti-Semite whose best friend

is named Halevi describes
woman as the curse

of wise men but hangs out
in brothels sketching

the hilarity and sadness
of whores sprawled

on a couch in the salon
waiting for patrons in bowlers

sporting trim mustaches
like his own or celebrating

the Madame's birthday
all this loose flesh

in long stockings around
the seated figure

of a tonsured woman
in a black dress

who might be the prioress
of a nunnery if not

for the image of a *poule*
scratching her ass

or another one sinking
into a mattress

as though she were melting
a peculiar nakedness

that makes us feel something
inviolable in its rawness

Keith Holyoak
2012 Foreigner

CLIMBING ABOVE
RONGBUK MONASTERY

A golden spire
draped with prayer-flag rainbows
and Qomolangma
burnished by summer snows

Point the way upward
beyond the human world—
the air gets thinner,
the end of the earth draws close.

Nothing but ice,
and rock, and wind, and sky—
life colors have vanished,
even the green of moss.

Gasping for breath
I crawl on hands and knees—
between bare stones
a purple blossom grows.

THE BODY GEOGRAPHIC

I rest my head
against the slope of her shoulder
and hear
the Amazonian confluences
where float
the pirogues of undiscovered tribes.
Her forests
are peopled
with people
whose names are unknown
whose languages
to our ears
are as the songs of birds.
Beyond the dunes of her breasts
the Mongolian steppes
are crossed
and recrossed
by caravanseries
who leave no trace in the grass.
I gaze
down the trackless miles of her legs,
over the boulders of her ankles,
to her feet,
those refugees
who have trekked
long miles to get here
bearing
the polished amber of her callouses.

But I am distracted from my admiration,
for she speaks
and I hear the strum
of her Abyssinian lutes.
Above these, rises
the catacombic vastness of her brain
with its Mandarin complexity
of caves and recesses.
Within resides
continuously chanting
a single
tiny
Taoist nun.

BURIANA BEACH

the tall weeds
weathered white
a screen behind the horse
nuzzling at grass fringe
on which the fieldhand put son
and the horse stepped
dignified up and down the beach

past the German girl in bikini
whose sex   later
bare backed he must have felt
—astride him
her beauty was unmistakable
and when the horse reared, the very image of mounting,
as she on him—
forelegs and cock
flailing air—
this
        she held to
—

sun up
the keels of the boats up
the men sleep under
eyes and cockpits
of those open boats

turned from sky—a blue
one cannot know
and not return to
—so easily tossed
in sea

I was told hardly any
learn to swim, they go out too far…night
…anguish…
to try
to make it back"

the old men
the survivors
they come to live in daylight
mending nets
or older
sitting quietly on the Paseo
shielding their eyes
from the sun   or what?

      Trying to put one and one together. Stranger. They
to me and vice-a-versa. Add the caves—confront the fact
that the real meaning of the cave is necessarily obscure. The
stranger makes it quite evident that he or she is different. The
commonality—if there is any—is in the primary roots, per-
haps hidden in the cave. The base from which the passions
extend? Undifferentiated? Peirce says: we are individuals only
as a result of error. So are we separate because we do not

acknowledge what a phenomenon like the caves might tell us? Or do we study them only to convert the caves, to normalize them into facts. Arranging the data scientifically, installing the *Son et Luminaire* which prettifies. A Hollywood cave, not one bit real.

An olive grove above town. Surrounding one side, an old rough sandstone wall, no mortar. The stones rest on one another as though held by indentations. On the other side of the wall, a deep gorge. One can see a foot path twisting down one side to a small stream—mercury where it catches light as it darts among the shrubs. No clouds. Sun, sun, sun stamping out a one-sided rhythm, maddening until one learns to live with it.

On the packed earth at the base of the wall, a lizard. The sheen of its body—a fabricated look as though in appearance a creature spanning two worlds, the natural and the artificial. The lizard, active all day and immobile in the cold nights.

I dwell on mutual estrangements. The locals give presents to us. Our landlady sent her servants with baskets of baked sweet potatoes, each the size of a melon. In the fields, the workers offer some picked piece of fruit or vegetable. We try to give something back, but are always refused. Are we friends with these people? No real intimacy. But we and the other *estranjeros* are keenly observed, talked about, become sources of humor for the locals. If I walk down the street with a puzzled look on my face, immediately someone will come up to me and point out where my wife is. And we talk about them, these mutual behaviors are a kind of exchange.

264

No real fondness for the caves. The government has spent a good deal of money putting in multi-colored lighting which throw varying pastel hues on the stalactites or give a half-hidden nook a soft glow. The lighting has made the cave pretty but stolen its stark, confrontational power, the experience of what it might be like to see it as though a seed-memory, a prime datum of our mental history. There was domesticity here, urns and pots, now placed in the little museum by the cave's entrance. They murdered here too. They slept, they shit, they made love. And the lights seem to efface all that.

WEST RIVER

Although some have remained,
most have moved, far from West River,
back East to the Dakota that lies
off the Missouri. East to land black
with furrows or thick with wheat.
Land so flat it slices off angles at horizon.

Further East to Mitchell, Yankton,
Elkton, South Shore. Where houses sit
on tracts cheek-to-jowl; quarter
acres reduced to nickel sized
gardens filled with snap peas
and rhubarb, marigold and memory.

People sit on porches or in parlors
with upright pianos and rockers covered
with comforters. They close their eyes,
yearn to remember what it is like
tonight in West River. West where bluffs
keep watch on the Missouri, west

past Murdo where the earth knobbed
with bumps and freckles and sunspots
burns to August brown. Where grass,
sparse and starved, gasps
for water, yielding to constant
wind; sometimes a whisper,

often a muffled sob, but then hissing
hard threats when it learns that it is not
the center of attention. Raising Cain,
raising dust, this land spewing
itself, propagating. Dust begetting
dust, until it becomes reborn

as yellow grit air. Much later,
that night, a lifetime from now,
West River people will lie
beneath a cold, white moon,
tucked away in skeletons
that used to be towns, dead

places like the light
years that grow between stars.
They will hold their breath
and listen East, trying to recall
a place where rain touches skin,
falling thick with gardens and wheat.

KADOKA

In Kadoka, South Dakota,
the main business of town is dying.
The worn-out, flat-front, sand-stone
stores huddle and shield
their faces from a constant,

grinding wind. The town lists
to railroads, its back pressed
flush to rusting tracks, waiting
for trains that won't come anymore.
Out from Kadoka, the ribbon roads

crease black and empty fields,
land so flat you can drop a line
and weight and come up plumb
crazy from the straightness of it all.
Those roads run east to the end

of town where buildings straggle
and fade into fence posts and winter
wheat. Or west, past where the town
used to be, out to the highway lined
with truckstops full of placemat ads

for Yogi Bear Campgrounds and Badland Motels.
The graduating class, reduced to twelve,
drive dusty brown beaters or trucks tuned
to the country station in Pierre, heading
to Denver or Cheyenne, or wherever

there's work. Old people sit and watch
blacktop roads buckle and roll
against August. They count time
by quarter hours and moons and look
out to the place where sky and ground meet.

SONNET TO GREEN

Astounding pale green garden—6 a.m.—
it glistens after last night's steady rain.
Each leaf's a faint yet brilliantly green gem
by moisture set translucently aflame;
as if the sun were rising from within
each tissue—not just spreading like a stain
from some remote horizon banked with cloud;
as if light were green seed, and not bright shroud.

This morning yellow's green, and blue is green,
and brown and black and white and gray grow green.
This morning green is greener. Not a sound
except the threat of thunder, and the round
of water dripping leaf to leaf, from green
to green, from green to green to green to green.

(Petulu, Bali—1997)

DEATH VALLEY

Silence absorbs the reach. The whiteness
of these salt flats tends to emptiness.
Sky scans, seeps into the great distance.

Lie like the burdens of rock, christened
into a furious rusk, breeched
into crystallized counterparts,
glistening like mica,
be like the sense of this silence,
itself unsure of itself.

Now along the casual main grain
we find perhaps the striations
in the surface, forwarding a new face
whose sculpture is etched
into a view salt-licked
that embraces
that desolate ground space
as more likely than any
other feature or future that the rain-
soused mind could grow or imagine.

We reel in the expanse and find
masks discarded on the mountains.

Gods of rock found eternal time
to masquerade as the land they created
here. Homage to their work
is the etchings we leave as footprints,
as lived markers, as signatures
that express our silent appreciation
of craft resembling nature.

BURGESS FALLS, TENNESSEE

— to j.w.l.

Where the waters cut the gorge cut strata of soft stone where granite
resists and holds itself against the water

where the waters drop in sheets across the rock steps then plunge
in white cascades

like moving ice the liquid of glacial rumbling froths and pounds
stone a heavenly and timeless pressure

the pull of the spin of the moon the star rise the unfathomable
magnetism of polar caps stretching the planet

there beside this monument of the elements we sit
father and daughter in the misted air

miraculous as geology, as history in stone that survives
that we have survived our lives.

Water is clear and moves and you see through turbulence
the struts and buttresses

granite and shale holding up the pounding of dropping water
the skeletal arches cradling

the pounding heart and still peer with the unchanged look of a
wordless infant watching

now with words across time where air and water and stone
become ideas

a woman writes philosophy where elements of truth and ethics,
the construction of worlds, are ideas

living off the page as real as the water falling and the mists rising
here capturing light

where surgent waters have cut away the earth
we sit centuries below the surface.

There's light and reflection, sound and respite from sound
and a moment's pause together.

The silver-bottomed leaves of the nearby willows turn to tell us
more about the mists and breezes that pass

as if all the lives that have made us packed into the helixes
of our genes come unsprung

dozens of relatives are watching us murmuring questions
in many languages the rabbi

the pharmacist from Minsk the dime-store merchant from Brooklyn
the venetian-blind maker from Jersey

all with held breaths perplexed trying to explain
the origins of this scholar

who has hiked a gorge with her father in Tennessee—
oh child.

PLAGIARIST

Consonants click in my consciousness
like castanets,
these are mine, but I don't want them;

what I want
is the slow, steady sound
of a horses' heart-beat
luscious land
I've never traveled to,

rural Ohio, perhaps
where calves are birthed beautifully
behind the barn.

I want to be
on the farm,
allow the boys
to burst through my body
and bleed me dry.

I will journey there
even if there is no plane;
I will sail with the wind of your words
and claim them
as my own.

BORDER CLASHES

We stroll out of El Zocalo
to find a world turning white
with snow. Not more than an hour ago,
or so it seems, it was still just a neighborhood
of homemade heaps and small dark houses
huddled against the single-digit skies
of southwest Detroit.

Kim plods to his Escort.
I fire up the Tempo,
turn on the wipers.
1-75 to the Lodge,
I pretend to follow the north star
but pull off at the Warren-Forest exit
and pull into the Third Street Saloon.
I take out a five for a Stroh's
and take a look around
at the only other patrons,
a table of students,
one of whom I know, a poet.
She catches my eye, looks away,
carelessly laughing as I recall

*

Christmas night at the Detroit-
Windsor border. I sat alone
in the back of an Accord
being driven by Mary, Katie
beside her, two sisters,
nearsighted, brown-haired, blond.
The guard bent down, jerked his head
my way, and sneered, "You gals
bringing anything across?"
Flashing licenses and teeth—
"Is—that–all?"—
Katie, enraged, swore for hours,
but how could I, I who have always
lived between countries,
between that night and another night,
thirteen years before,
when my girlfriend and I
found ourselves detained by Customs
because I was said to resemble
a West Indian brother
twenty years my senior?

Later, back in the U.S.A.,
Katie and I danced our asses off.
Sweat flung from the sprinkler
our figures cut, twinkled like icy
stars on the stage
lit unlit by slo-mo strobes.
I could smell the sweat of a hundred
worlds, the sweet and sour stench
of cheap perfume and bargain-brand soap.
It was the hot sauce and garlic of Hamtramck
and Highland Park, Rayis Brothers

and Brothers Barbecue, Eastern Market
and Lafayette Coney, an ethnic festival
teeming with bloods.

When the lights came up, we filed out,
stunned, as though the places
to which we had to return–
Plymouth and Detroit–had been found dead
in each other's arms:
murder-suicide.

*

Last call, and I'm just fine.
I stumble to my car, spin out
of the lot in a spray of sleet and mud
and hit the northbound Lodge at sixty.
Not a few of these vehicles are harboring drunks
like me. The world is still turning white.
The white dotted lines are useless now.
We weave our ways home,
as best we can,
in lanes of our own making.

LIFE IN THE ORDOVICIAN

What vision brought him
While brooming last year's leaves
Off the trod
Limestone of his garden's path:
The crazy-quilt of its lithograph
A Chinese scroll
That patterns chaos with its forms–
Unrolled inked petroglyphs,
Rubbings from the ancient
Bone-houses of the corals–
The old of the daily news printed
On the crinoid's static, vertebraeic stems,
Their broken, vertiginous anemone blooms
Wavering in the shallows
Of a four hundred million year old sea.
Which begs the question of
Not how, but when,
Having already long ago vanished,
What end there is in sight?
For the work, the path he follows
To sweep, or to be swept along
Clay banks millennia deep,
Older than the river and that river's life
At one with the constancy of its purl.
Time flows in the moment
As perennial as the peonies he tends,
Rooted, and just as tenacious
As the surrounding oaks

That make a Jacob's ladder for the ants,
Out-lasting all with a name who live here.
And he, doing just as they who came before,
At play in the role of gardener,
With the gardener in the usual of his weeds,
Taking care to serve.
Almost as if the flower
Existed for the man in him alone
To bend to—
Praise requiring nothing of summer
Except a sometimes rain,
And the cold enough of winter
With a little faith to breathe in—
The air of its own accord
Carrying the sweet
Scent of flowers beyond a human use,
As was said to be carried
Believer to belief,
Rumurous, on the wings of angels—
Or failing that, on the stubborn backs
Of an everyday human grief.
And though borne with a bearer's
Grace to believe,
The whole of him no more than they,
Than last year's leaves, the dust he clears
And through the clearing sees
The path over which the broom whispers:
The stray of its binding mortars, the shifting
Chronologies of its broken shores—
Atlantean shale's shattered spindrift ruins
Proleptic with the sacred truths.
Beneath his feet the toppled
Ashlars of its crazy-quilt.

The pre-marmoreals of its salt intaglios–
The varietal weathers of its aquatints,
Escalloped bone-alphabets
Still in the making of its runes.
And he now on his knees,
His hands in the sensitive splay
Of a blind man's fingers,
Taking its pulse,
Listening for his own heart's beat
In those many dead oceans,
His one good ear pressed to the floor of the world.

PHILOSOPHICA

WHY DOGS ARE BETTER THAN PEOPLE

Because they are.

Because they are not cats.

Because they have no theories,
and never weary me
with talk of rights, self-
esteem, or some such
metaphysical crap.

Because they like the way things smell
and never pretend they don't.

Because, for dogs,
everything,
every moment,
even this one,
is their favorite,

and when told
not to bark,

they still do.

VALEDICTION
FOR JARA BONNER

" 'Two winged companions,' says an Upanishad, '
two birds are on the branch of a tree. One eats the fruit the other looks at it.'
These two birds are the two parts of our soul."
Simone Weil

Of the two kinds of bird,
one that stares and one that eats,
there is a third
feathering the nest,
darning sky and field.

Of the kinds of bird
one eats one stares
and from afar the third
offers thrilling song:

May you hear it always.

WHAT QUESTION

What Question
Does the bee
Continually pose
To the flower
Whose answer
Is always sweetness

BEE SEASON

– for my mother

Nectar-driven day burns down to evening
as light-swarms crumble to ash, vanish with day,
and endless summer, at its height, is leaving.

The goldenrod, from gold to rust, is grieving,
and sky, gunmetal blue, weathers to gray.
Nectar-driven day burns down to evening.

There must still be a teeming hive, we sing,
where mothers show their sons an easier way
of leaving summer at its height of leaving.

A door must open high up in the ceiling
of the sky, a crack through which bees slip away
as nectar-driven day burns down to evening

and life splits open like a trunk, heaving
sweetness on the earth. We stop and pray
for endless summer, but amber light is leaving,

tearing itself from limbs and leaves. The breathing
canopies, stripped down now, whisper: *stay.*
But nectar-driven day burns down to evening,
and endless summer, at its height, is leaving.

STANDING ALONE

Have you been out
On a moonlit night
Before the fields
Have grown into themselves
When they are still
Vast acres of possibility
And you can see yourself standing
Beneath the gray blue moon
In the middle of those possibilities
Not the self that is
But that other grayer self
Standing alone in the fields

MAN IN HAT

we knew

what was coming
so did She

fat train bearing down
and no de-rail in sight

shook the ground
for miles around

shook the thistle
and the briar

shook the willows, too

man in gaudy hat
sat at rail's end

met that fat
head on

THE PAGE-TURNER

is understood to be invisible,

perched beyond the lowest octave,
poised, a tense handmaiden, eyes
faithful to the score, ready to release
the hands clenched

prayerfully in her lap. Pizzicato
cello-strings quiver. Violin-
and viola-bows leap up, a trio of shuttles
warp-weaving,

the pianist's fingers threading the weft.
Now the notes are running out of room,
she leans, then she thrusts
a bare arm out

into the loom's fabric, her fingers
seize the recto corner and freeze.
Perilous moment! We are not meant to notice
her, the rapt gaze

fastened on her maestro's face,
waiting for that cue, impersonal —
curt nod, lofted eyebrow, even a deeper
breath — that gives

permission to the page-turner, that says
Now I need you!, and she performs
so swiftly, all elegance and clarity
in the turning,

accomplished. Then tacet once more,
waiting, returned beyond the lowest
possibility of sound, to listen,
to watch. As we watch

what is woven yet can't be seen,
the beauty calling the quintet
and us to gather — all unseen.
We go home,

make our customary mistakes, confuse
visible signs with invisible grace.
But as sleep deranges us, perhaps
we hear the tapestry

and glimpse a silent turning of the page.

THE MERIT OF
THE DELICATE ANIMAL

It is not by your merit that the sun shines on you. And it is not by your merit that the rain falls on you. Rather it is by the merit of the delicate animal. —*Traditional*

This one's not chosen, is left
to find its way apart from
the herd at the roadside,
milling rump to rump. This goat
presses its length to a wall,
slowly raises its head so the throat
is exposed, shivers and trots
into stillness the tapping hooves break.

The goatherd places his staff
like a pole to order the rubble and stalks:
here, the shell of a stove,
there, the yellow grasses,
each shoot a single torch brightening
the distance from heaven to flowers.

ABEL'S BLESSING

Abel placed the newborn lamb at the teat.
He offered grain in his hand

and patted its matted flank
until it grew large and followed the herd

though Abel remembered the markings,
could pick out the one among many.

He pressed its head to his hip
then bound the yearling ram,

stabbed it as if the wound were his own
and the cutting brought him peace:

the body undone,
intimate memory freed

in blood over fist-shaped stones
pulled from the hillside

where sheep lipped air
as if the manna fell even then

from heaven anchored by sand
in pillars, held upright

by wind. They were not
to be closed within walls, not

climbed except by a boy
who killed what loved him

and set it on fire. He
loved the beast he'd slain.

So God saw Himself
in Abel's face.

ANSWER TO SIMMIAS

> Simmias, if I remember rightly, has fears and misgivings
> whether the soul, being in the form of harmony,
> although a fairer and diviner thing than the body,
> may not perish first.   —Plato, *Phaedo*

This happened to me once: I wrote a chaconne
for orchestra (these were my student days),
I scored the thing, took pains, and heard my phrases
begin to soar above their grounded bass.
And then I lost the pages, God knows how.
Those precious, scribbled staves just disappeared
beneath the waves of senior-year disorder.
I wasn't daunted, though. I could still hear it,
the music in my "head," my "thoughts," my "mind":
unscientific terms: had I dropped dead
that day, the probing scalpels would have failed
to find a single quaver in my brain.
Yet they were there, I heard it, wrote it down
again — improved it, even, took it closer
to what I had in mind.
                        Now please imagine
your soul as music. You live out your years
becoming rhythm, harmony, the structure
of what you are. Then comes the final measure,
the whole-note rest of death. The printed score —
your blood and bones and breath and DNA —
will decompose, will disappear as quickly
as my first-draft chaconne. What of the music?
How can you live again? A greater mind
must needs remember you and let you play

296

forever, each thematic line perfected
and finally sounding true. Heaven is sounding
impossible these days, with every quantum
of matter mathematically weighed and accounted for.
But it's no more, or less, miraculous
than what I have in mind.
                                        And so, *da capo*:
the choirmaster smiles and gives the downbeat,
the angels pluck you out upon their lyres
while voices far more absolute, more lovely
than any you imagined sing the burden,
as light as life. Simmias, let us pray:
Remember us, O Lord. Keep us in mind.

Lianne Spidel
2012 Pairings

CONJECTURE

A tapestry makes sense to some
when all of us will fit
into a silken landscape
that explains everything—
I a glint in the river, you
a stone in the turret of a castle.

Some find a labyrinth likely,
envisioning a maze where escape
is the answer rather
than the trees themselves,
the new bloomings and small
losses gathering underfoot.

While theories thrive and falter,
I lean toward the leaves,
curling and going to lace,
veins green and insistent
even as they fall, toward
the ridges of a coral sunset

smudged by an unseen thumb,
toward the magnolia, fragrant
and ancient, the patterned
giraffe with his high
blood pressure, the peacock
sweeping his art deco tail

298

across the dust, all
left with us, haphazard
in profusion—seed and blossom
cloudbank, beast and bird—
keeping their secrets, free
to find their way.

PARTY CLOTHES

"Eternity is in love with the forms of time." Joseph Campbell

Life is like that floral-patterned
see-through blouse I wore once
to a party where the light was dim.
It wasn't till I danced with someone
that he saw through it and stared.
Life, the teaser, dresses like that
and all the forms of time want to dance.
Then dancing, looking through
to naked shape, look further still:
seeing breasts—flesh's fruit—
see how, ripe, they contain their own decay,
how joy and sorrow come of the same thing,
are the same thing, only separated briefly
to be partners for this dance.

AN AUGUST DAY
IN THE IDEAL CITY

The ideal city is a hill town
where ramparts
afford spectacular views
of orchards and vineyards
and in the distance
a chain of mountains
where, year after year,
a bumper crop of boletes is found.

The hill is steep.
There is no place for outskirts.
One is either in or out;
on the road or off it.
Comings and goings
are known for hours in advance,
and mourned for hours after.
Dust rises from the road
like smoke from a stick of incense
and the wanderer's mother
begins to dice an onion
as the setting sun
tints distant glaciers
the color of apricots.

There are no monsters
at the heart
but a square

bisected by the shadow
of a castellated tower.
Smaller shadows loiter
behind couples on the promenade–
the two a boneless negative space
without knuckles going white.

The ossuaries are stacked
with the bones of intact families
and during siesta
only thunder rattles the windows.
There will be seasons of apples and truffles;
seasons of the daffodil
and the iris and the sunflower.
Storks will nest
unmolested on the spires
and the arrow of geese in flight
will be the point
where parallel lines meet.

The language will preserve
at least two forms of the pronoun you:
a formal form, an informal
and quite possibly a third
reserved for those no longer with us,
for those we long for
even if we knew them
only for a moment
in the parking lot
of the Chateau Marmont.

There should be myriad forms:
one form for each one
of our friends and intimates,
for each acquaintance and relation,
that makes our relationships explicit,
even to those that overhear us,
and those listening in,
as the tower's shadow takes aim
at that swept and watered square
a hundred years from tomorrow.

MT. AUBURN CEMETERY

Enduring trees
and grounds are luxuriant this autumn
as they will be every season,
as if the dead deserve all the best
of this world after they leave it;
as if the living, charmed by nature's generosity
(the grandeur of a beech), should, reflecting,
grow more reconciled to mortality.

We are a deciduous race, destined
to shed out of time leaves,
to surrender obsolete selves.
Our hearts are pith, archives
of desire quick and quickening,
and you and I walk these shaded paths
holding hands, tendrils
of our late, regenerate love.

TWO POEMS ABOUT ZHAO ZHOU

A monastic asked Zhao Zhou, "What is the meaning of the Ancestor's
coming from India?"
Zhao Zhou said, "The cypress tree in the garden."
The monastic said, "Master, please don't teach using an object."
Zhao Zhou said, "I am not showing an object to you."
The monastic said, "What is the meaning of the Ancestor's coming from India?"
Zhao Zhou said, "The cypress tree in the garden."

MY ANSWER
TO ZHAO ZHOU'S TREE

Using dead reckoning we travel
from polestar to Antares
looking down, falling,
finding earth. And we
are born again, exchanging
fluids first, then gas, then
information. The touch,
whether chemical or
chimerical, makes us whole.

Meanwhile, Zhao Zhou's
tree remains, though now
it is made of iron: Where
has all the wood gone?
Zhao Zhou knew:
he could not cut it down.
Its shadow covers Altair
and smoky nebulae,

Andromeda and heartbeat.
It covered Zhao Zhou's sleep
and it covered Gautama's mouth
so no words could come out.

We think and we talk.
We walk unexpectedly
because we are expected to:
children get up and sing.
We think we are walking
into something but we
are walking into nothing.
No words or sounds point
our way or show our way.
Blackbirds take the place
of leaves in the high branches
of the hickory in winter.

MY OTHER ANSWER

Some people are generous
and kind. I am not. I
am competitive and often
unkind. Knowing this, can
I change my ways?
So he said: The cypress
tree in the garden.

It is said that the Buddha
is a sixteen foot or eight foot
golden body. There is
fog on the snow.

The Buddha's frozen hands
connect in a circuit
of fingers the future
and past cannot contain.
I notice a bit of snow like
a tiny sail on the statue
of Buddha's sea.

The young monk said
to Zhao Zhou: why meditate?
Why put one foot in
front of the other? Why
cross the threshold,
the lintel, why stand
under the chupa,
why spin the record,
run the fingers along
the fretboard, follow
desire, or not, or
lift the stone to
make memorial, heavy
and dense over
the freshly dead?

Zhao Zhou looked
the other way,
toward the courtyard
outside the gate,
beyond the emissary
who came and taught
him the sacred
finger dance, the circuit,
the orb beyond

supposing, the shape
that looks like a heart.
He swallowed his
past and future thoughts,
not generous, not kind.
Turned away.

THESE PETTY PRODUCTS
OF MAN

These petty products of man,
metaphysical systems,
how might they do justice to God?

Metaphysics must be biography –
to merge with God
rather than suffer
his dictates –
this is the Puritan fervor –

The end of all art
is not the art object,
it is the man redeemed,
the supreme work of art –

It will arrive unannounced
and from a religious heart
and make beautiful
the railroad car, the
galvanic battery, the
electric jar, the mills
& machinery –

The mercenary impulse
and the Marxists
are just as unholy,
an ignoble and vulgar service –
Satanic finance –
an aimless nation
of incurable distortions

THE WANDERER

"All the rivers run into the sea; yet the sea is not full . . ."

(Ecclesiastes 1:7)

Slowly the seasons circle and converge.
Summer's assumptions fall beneath the surge
Of wind that widens in its withering.
Late-winter blurring into early-spring
Summons the Wanderer in his own blood,
Bursts through whatever bulwarks had withstood
The pulse of passion rushing to the void –
Till all delineations are destroyed.

Why should the Wanderer pursue his course,
Season by season, searching for a source,
And slowly circle like an old refrain
From east to west and west to east again –
Summer to autumn; autumn, winter; spring –
If nothing comes of all his wandering?

He sees the seasons circling back once more,
And nothing is as it has been before
Upon the lands and in the skies and seas;
He sees how in their superfluities
They seize the allotted moment and withdraw,
Accommodated to the common law
That binds them up as sheaves beneath the sun
And sweeps them out – into oblivion.

Our life is error, then, the Wanderer says.
It bears us fiercely forward through the days,
Faithful to some unerring symmetry.
Green burns gold and burnishes to red,
And imperceptibly is blurred and bled,
Falling at last beneath the ancient tree.

HOMESICK FOR HEAVEN

1.

Because there is no rain in the land
Because there is too much rain in the land

The exiles return—

But as always?
Or just so far?

Do they wade in the shallow waters
Do they wait for tsunamis

Or those Santa Ana winds?

Do they wander out of gratitude
Toward and from the currency of duty

Or does the distance between the circle and spiral

Spiral out of the thought of nothing
Out among the stars growing

Small and faint to one another?

* * *

Because can only tell a story, the k of
Aka as KS, or natural

Selection, or luck—

Platitudes
Of levelers.

Say the earth explodes inside a world
Say a world much like the world that dies

Is born in blood, an alphabet we read

Left to right and right to left.
What remains unsaid is written
Asymetrically: recto v. verso.

2.

For example breaches the circle cited:
They who stand and wait, step, wait,
                              each step
An installment on the rights to copies
Of the stations they repeat in slow
                              motion.
Given the anomaly of no parking
Spaces I prophesied—that is—inferred
                              an event,
Excess, a hairline fracture in the integrity
Of the everyday. One might say I saw
                              them there
Just before I chanced to cross the line

Staggered up and down a flight of stone—
                    spinal cord
Of a back so long and wide those little
Crosses inching forward, up, were not
                    a cross
Nor a hindrance to my lunch with a woman
Whom I might have walked with in a world

                    unpromised

Not unlike the world from which I fell

Like a stone dislodged from that stone-set face.
What is left behind will yet serve:

                    a doorway

Not unlike an open mouth: a tongue

Sticking out to receive the little crosses—
Or a river of spittle: frozen-over

                    invective.

                    * * *

She went straight to dessert, her laughter descending

Like a dove plunging out of the sky—

                    lovers after

315

All when all this passes away

                    as promised.

3.

Because there is no sun
Because there are only stars

I am walking toward the only light
I cannot see, a theory of noon in my head,
Stump pain in the absence of a stump

I am following the north star—
Or is it only Alpha Centauri?

Dawn awaits and beckons like Venus de Milo
As I fall forward out of history
Under the Order of African Mysteries:

How to break the law and raise the dead
How to meld forks into measuring spoons

How the circulation of desire
Overrides the law of circuit/circuit-
Breakers. How the house of language flares:

Blood in the face: a burning bush: the door
Locks and unlocks from the inside only. Inside
There are only replicas of Venus de Milo

Or it's time to place this land in order
On the Order of the Solar Temple

Time to turn this star into a sun
With a bullet to the back of the head—
For the flesh is weak. Almost Heaven

Comes in peace and friendship. How to carry,
Draw and hold at bay the flux and flotsam

Deemed the world. He which is half-flesh
Draws and quarters land into human plots.
The eschatology of if-then

Presupposes nothing after, nothing other
Than the missing matter of the universe:

Father—or the four quarks, the dark
Link that yokes apes to zoos, or apes to stars
Farther and farther apart. Why have you?

4.

Because we live
    in the Land of Point
the evil Count and Oulipo
    exchange rings
in a clearing of the Pointless Forest
    and settle down
in a bottomless NORC
    called No Return.

Because we live with Arrow
    and Oblio
death always arrives
    a little early
and we point back
    to incomplete dreams
or point out
    unkept vows
our point being
    because the absurd.

5.

Because you gave your word
                    you had no right
to take his life
            you should have come
and testified
        how he destroyed
year after year
            we would have listened
to believe
        not that we
accept your human
            testimony
without certain
            stipulations
he through you
        fails to meet.
Whom did you see
        how did you know
was it him
        we don't believe

a word you say
          why would he
appear to you
          when it was us
who walked with him
               who know his ways
how he goes
          and goes on

6.

like a boy
          and his dog
or a dog
          and his boy

Who return to the fold as former exiles
Repatriated through the spires and steeples

Of the city and the City of God.
Church is a varied one-storey building

Where the wheat is gathered and stored in bundles:
Visionary tongues by turns sinister, sappy,

Second-run features in a multiplex.
Trade is a varied one-storey building

like a boy
        playing fetch
with his dog
        or a dog
playing possum
            with a boy

or a treed boy

abandoned dog

7.

You are authentic in the folds of meaning
Which is always and only heavenly meaning

Not this pious authenticity
Subsidized by figurines of King

Or the King—or the King of Kings.
You will follow the scent of a slain panther

As supreme truth descends like incense
You will never smell. Subways hurtle

Toward the nothing which is not yet
Possible. A new sun, a new earth

Unintelligible. Insensible. Blessings
Under insufficient stars or suns:

So many lights—so many light-years.
There, ahead, the mute messiah waits

Curled like a leaf in his wheelchair.
Yes, yes, he can hear our prayers

But he cannot answer. Go to him.
Press your lips to his. Breathe. Lay

Hands on him. Raise him from his throne.
Send him on his way, grateful, astonished.

8.

Where we are going God cannot come.
When I was a child. Not that the child
Was spared blindness and instantly killed
By lightning but that the father turned
In time to see. Flying saucers
Are time machines, they transport the child
Cowering in a corner of a loud house
To a world once removed from the house
Called the Law of Turning and Returning
To a book called Was. Turn the page
And the book gets bigger, a monster
Every child will learn to fear,
Learn to laugh at with its body,
Fat, resilient, shitting, teething.

9.

What we are going to become
God cannot.

      So it is written
In the dust of the Law we scatter

Like stars or motes over our eyes.
Somthing else means most or least.

Not that a child is spared blindness
When his heart suddenly stops.

Where we are going God cannot go
Unless we put a bullet in the back

Of his head. Let him walk with us.
First one on their knees is home.

PHILOLOGICA

WORDSPLAY

She speaks. Fingers
on the tone holes
of her clarinet—breathy whooos coaxing chords
into controlled motion.
We form
our g's and d's, our f's,
our k's, comma'd, coma'd, a period, a question
      in the ease of a breath. I have seen
a word,
      The Word, a whirl, the lift
of a staff part the sea, construct a wall, form
a pillar, cause a lamb to acquiesce. I have seen
a word quiet
      a word,
splitting a tongue in two, splitting a tongue into
the splitting of words. I have seen words escape
from your sleep,
      your deep,
          your words
that would stop a train, derailed, a failed engine, an engineer,
a failed trip, a split rail. I have seen
my words
      buzz around
my head like killer bees, cross the tract of no-man's-land,
      the DMZ,
push themselves into tremors, my cavity
coaxing the round of an O, the W-H of why. Even
a chirping baby will push his pink tongue in and out,

                    trying to wet the reed
            of his clarinet.

            The yogi master says
        to place the tongue softly against the roof
        of your mouth to keep the rabid mind
        from speaking out, from forming the glottal vowels
        of worry, from jumping with the lingual jump rope
        on the long journey
                    toward the far-away place
                            of your Absolute, toward becoming
                                    your perfect dumb self.

YOUR HANDWRITING

As the anniversary of your death nears,
I feel the pull to see your handwriting, hold

papers you pressed pens against, read
your words, the ways you formed

letters in journals, notes on beloved
books, prayers you wrote.

You braid cursive with printed
letters that slant like calligraphy.

Your *P* in **Peace** plump as a down pillow,
and like Emily, your capitalization never standard.

Your *n* mimics a *u*.
When a word begins with *d*,

as in *dwell*, you form a flat, straight staff
but when at word's end, as in *surround*,

the staff's fat as a baseball bat, and instead of lilting
right, it leans left as if to shield letters beneath it.

Sometimes you break words—
stre tch, Kind ness, brea the.

I mouth them, touch their wings and sutures. You
lean near, and I divine the deep murmur of your voice.

VICTOR WEAVE

Call the hearth at home friendly fire
Call the cold hours' starlight friendly fire
& while friendly fire's everywhere & forever
this fire reaps & preys
this fire lights both ways

Mine eyes flake with unexploded impact

Mine eyes infiltrate jellied tank towns
power walking well-heeled graft
along sweat-banded loopy beachheads

Call the pain of birth friendly fire
Call the cries of babes friendly fire
& while friendly fire's everywhere & forever
this fire gives & takes away
this fire leaps & falls both ways

Mine eyes belly up to the guile larder
guild guilt & fool around

Mine eyes climb hand over hand
collateral pig's foot caked
camel spit in the pentagon pool

Call the threaded looms friendly fire
Call our darkened room friendly fire
& while friendly fire's everywhere & forever
this fire flays & it slays
this fire weaves both ways

Mine eyes elope with pack rats
reckless shuttlecocks are mine eyes

Mine eyes field strip jackets whisker-coned
ambulatory un-deloused starvation buffer
bubs of trench flag bridges downed

Call lakes when they shine friendly fire
Call waves when they break friendly fire
& while friendly fire's everywhere & forever
this fire aches & it craves
this fire bathes both ways

Mine eyes have seen shroudy captives file
down choked dune-tides that bind

Mine eyes align beloved warps click-beetled
below bellowing hypno-stipulative pushovers
registering duality-crest bledfellows

329

Call grasses when they sway friendly fire
Call fireflies in their dance friendly fire
& while friendly fire's everywhere & forever
this fire burns where it braves
this fire churns both ways

Mine eyes are incandescent lusty fleas
procreant witnesses swallowed by the sword

Mine eyes crosshair whole quilts of plague ghetto
ethers inhaled   stuttering grease clams
global intake cringe-roots, boot-lamped

Call the morning star friendly fire
Call the setting sun friendly fire
& while friendly fire's everywhere & forever
this fire eats the days
this fire bites both ways

Mine eyes muster the tar pits' babble
they savor lies seasoned & enshrined

Mine eyes hourglass nay-knowing cloverleafs
new-mown chopped quicksaw sanddust mounds
of crater-sculpt horizon ramps, offed

Call the comet's tail friendly fire
Call the new moon's silver friendly fire
& while friendly fire's everywhere & forever
this fire sleeps within the blaze
this fire wakes both ways

Mine eyes cook dawn's early light
& the smoke of twilight's fast breathing

Mine eyes lock headlong baggy & bodiless
consensus-swept support nodes
giddy on dire World Cop Love

Mine eyes whorl whorish ado & anon

HEX WORDS

Everywhere were jars and other containers, filled with various
herbs, stalks, blossoms, seeds   what appeared to be an entire
pharmacopoeia of country cures.   "What's that used for?"
            I inquired.   "For what ails you."

"How'd you come by that wart there?"

"O yes sir, you can hear it all right.
You come out with me one night next year -
don't smile, I'm not talkin' about country matters -
and you'll hear it too:
the softest rustle of leaf
soft as fairies' wings
and you know them stalks
is stretchin' up to the sky
the tassels is length'nin
the ears is bit by bit gettin' fatter
till you can hear their husks pop.
That's somethin'
on a hot dark night
standin' by the cornpatch
in the light o' the Mulberry
moon and hearin'
the corn grow."

You take as much
of this powder as the point
of your knife will hold

mix with one ounce
of good whiskey
and put it in a common
vial   make a hole
in the bee-hive and pour
a vision of the queen
of the underworld. Good
luck and more
to the point good riddance.

THE ABECEDARIAN

1.

He's like some
Aviator, flying high, rising above
Bees in girls' bonnets about settling down.
Caesar to his subjects, he demands strict
Dealings from those close to him—yet wants
Easy friendships, rejecting their depths with
Effusive excuses some swallow whole.
Genius of seductions, it's like shooting
'H', swelling intercourse into his own
Ideology, coming to feel the strength
Jason and his Argonauts or marines on
Caissons just rolling along must have used:
Elbow grease, real staying power, building
Empires of their own desires whenever
Entering capitals, issuing orders,
OD'ing at brothels while watching through
Peepholes all the bodily postures, hot
Cubicles filling with smoke—and only
Arsonists could create more messes from
Escapades of flesh, burning in those fires.
Tea-bags beneath his eyes, urinary and
Uterine tracts puffed up before him like
Viennese pastry, he'd eat them, seeing
Double, usually, at the inevitable
Executions attended often by
Wily commanders ready to catch some
Z's with the city's most beautiful daughters.

2.

              "Everything's
Aces, Ace," A. says when they go to bed.
Beatitude fills his head—but when he leaves
C-notes by her pillow, slipping out again,
Desensitized in the dawn, no longer so
Eager, he sees her poor black underwear,
Effervescent once, hanging over a chair—
G-string, garter-belt, bra—and needs some pure
H_2O to revive his spirits, dimmed
Eyeballs clouding over after hours of
Japeries at the clubs. He remembers
K.O.'ing some stranger for ogling her;
Elsewhere, they made out, rubbed together
Emery boards of skin, their polished nails
Ending up in their flesh, finding the best
Openings into bliss. Strutting their stuff,
Peacocks primping in their fanciest clothes,
Cute, they came on like that all night, sharing
Artifice so extreme, their style almost
Escalated them beyond the stares of
T-bone steak eaters in pubs where they played
Ukuleles, swayed to hulas, stamped plastic
Visas to pay for food. But now he feels
Doubly used, like being slapped by his mad
Ex-es in the backs of cocktail lounges,
Wise-ass kids in tow, all their patience at
Zero, telling him he'd better change his game.

3.

"I must change,
Eh? Okay, I'll try..." Reluctantly, but
Beetling brows softening, he thinks of calm
Seas rolling softly, shores forming a smooth
Detour from all those previous frenzied
Ecosystems turned to stagnant rivers,
Effluents draining to deltas, and exclaims,
"Gee!" disingenuously... Then it hits, an
H-bomb ready to drop like his pants for
Idylls with bodies naked and common as
Jaybirds in his city turned grey by decay.
Casing the joints, he might take the subway,
El, any means to meet new women packed
Em-spaces apart, or closer, like meat;
Any way to press his hot skin to them,
Opalescent vessels all dancing like
Peas in the pods of dark discotheques they
Queue up before after midnight each night,
Ardently wanting to join some movement,
EST, for example, which promises fun...
"Tea or hash," B. asks when he gets inside.
"You! I mean, both!" He takes a peek down her
V-neck-exposed chest as she leans with, "The
'Double' you ordered." She's quite the little
Exhibitionist, big breasts turning him on.
"Why can't I have her now?" he sighs. "It's ea-
Sy," his other self replies. He tries. Time flies...

4.

                    "From little
Acorns grow great big oaks," he tries to joke,
BVD's tightening as he peers through C.'s
See-through top. "Not just compensating for
Detumescence problems?" she replies,
Evening the score in their debate on
Efficacies of 'scoring.' "You'd be some
Genie if I rubbed you and you'd grant my wish,
Aitchbone, buttocks, on down." But, "What's the big
Idea?" she sneers, and he feels he's climbing
Jacob's Ladder, up to nothing, only
Catering to crotchets of her cool flesh,
Elevating his attitude beyond
Empathy with such desires. Falling back,
Enervated, his whole system brought down, no
Opiate he knows can get him up when her
Peevish persona leaves him high and dry,
Cumulatively clouded, like drafting
Armistice agreements with some stubborn
S.O.B. She'd like to see herself on
TV more than come to terms with him,
Using her fresh-faced yet power-tripping
V.I.P. position at the local station.
"W.H.O.R?" he asks, aiming for some
Expiation of his failed lust. "Am I too
Wired for you, perhaps?" she asks him, at the
Zenith of his fast-growing self-disgust.

5.

He takes an
Apolitical trip, making a quick
Beeline to London to catch the swinging
Scenery, dreaming of all the suppressed
Deviance he's heard of under the heading,
"English hospitality." He ignores
F-stops on his camera, shooting like a
G-man at D., a Cockney "bird" who drops
Aitches and panties for him in the end...
"I can't understand her," he thinks, later,
Jay-walking in Florence, "her food tastes like
K-rations, but she responds, 'The bloody
'Ell it does!'" Yet Europe's like Oz, Auntie
Em's back in Kansas, and he feels free to
Entertain himself as he may, as they say,
Owed this whirlwind tour... But, "Where do people
Pee around here?" he wonders, then takes his
Cue and does as Romans do: on the street! "They
Are demonstrative"—unlike at home, where, in
Essence, men's concerns seem to be how to
Tee off at the local club... Missing the old
U. S. A., he goes to Germany, where guides say,
"Ve vill zee ze offens now!" "Schnell! Schnell! On ze
Double, you hear!" in his head, it doesn't take
X-ray eyes to see past suffering humanity
Whining and dying... Drowning, the Zuider
Zee's underwater. Guards stop him at each border.

6.

He remains
Amiable, until he meets E. in France,
Beefy, yet pretty. He describes the hectic
Sequence of events that cut his trip short:
Devaluation of the dollar. She blames
Evil foreign policies, holding forth, but,
"F—- it," he says, pretending to take it all
Genially. Yet, it's hard, as when, in 4-
H Club, he was "Unlikeliest to Succeed,"
ID'ing a part of his personality,
Jaded, but still wanting transport from
Quays along the Seine flowing past the once-
Elegant boites where he'd gorge to forget
Emptiness for awhile. Forced to take an
Enema later at the hotel, the rank
Odors feed a sense he'd like to suppress:
Piqued at the slightest ripped fingernail or
Cuticle, the hordes of tourists forming
Armies forcing him from Paris just as his new
Escort wants to show its "grand human design,"
Teasing cultured taste, feeling perverse, as
Usual, he orders only water, drinks
Vichy instead of wine, with a scent he'd
Dub "Elusive Bouquet," spending a last few
Expurgated hours together, with their time
Winding down, no chance for more before, "Where eez
Zee passport, pleeze?" after a last kiss and squeeze.

7.

Back again,
Aching with lust, he goes to town to look for some
Beaver. On the plane he could hardly wait, hot
Semen backed up all the way. Finally, he finds a
D-cup-packing cutie. "Whuddlid be?" F.'s
Enunciation's terrible, but he doesn't mind
Effortlessly slipping into his car, stripping
Jeans off in seconds, his member rigid as an
H's bar between them as she grabs it and he
Eyes her: the best thing he's seen since landing at
J.F.K.! If only he saw he was breaking laws:
Que sera sera, she's only sixteen, barely past
Elementary school! But experienced,
Emptying his swollen balls as he drives...
Anyone can tell he likes breaking speed limits, too,
Over eighty, coming fast, stopping only for
Penile needs or fuel, crossing state lines with this
Cucumber-eater, open-mouthed whenever he's hard.
Arguing with himself, "She's a nymphet, nympho,
S-e-x written all over, jailbait to a
'T'." "But what's a guy to do?" He savors her
Youth—though they barely converse outside his
Vehicle... "If you keep her with you, she can
Double your pleasure when you go out to
X-rated movies or come home from workouts at the
'Y'. So, why worry?" She can't even talk when, with new
Zeal, he takes her someplace and again stuffs her face.

340

8.

        Reaching the
Apex of his lust, relaxed,
Beaming, pleased at last,
Seizures shake him like a
Demon when a toothsome
Eager grin over the lush
Efflorescence of his sex—
Jesus, O, Jesus, O, Jesus
H. Christ!—makes his wet
Eyes roll back like joyous
Jaycee's buttons, no longer
Capable of any thought or
Element of control: on an
Eminence, discovering new
Energies that her full mouth
Opens him into with a pure
Paean of praise for his tool,
Cue-stick well-handled by an
Artist of pool, liquid seeking
Estuary, flooding away all his
Teeming desire before a soft
Uvula, a quivering Mount of
Venus, as wet as they can get—
Doubled uvulas, lips, entered in
Ecstasy, flashing in black and
White like lightning brightening
Zebras in racing-striped flight.

ABOUT THE AUTHORS

MARY MARGARET ALVARADO is the author of *Hey Folly*. She was an Iowa Arts Fellow and Provost's Post-Graduate Writing Fellow at the University of Iowa, the writer-in-residence at Cincinnati's Seven Hills School, and a finalist for the 2014 Rona Jaffe. Her work has been published widely, notably in *The Beloit Poetry Journal*, *The Boston Review*, *The Kenyon Review*, and *The Iowa Review*. She lives in Colorado and goes by her nickname, Mia.

JOHN ANSON has worked as a psychologist, first as a therapist and currently as an expert witness in hearings held for involuntarily hospitalized patients. In the 1970s and 1980s, his poetry was published in a number of small literary magazines including Poetry (Chicago), *The Threepenny Review* and *Arizona Quarterly*. Books include a chapbook of his sonnets, *A Family Album* and from Dos Madres Press, his translation of *Les Trophées by José-Maria de Heredia* (2013) and *Time Pieces – poems & translations* (2014.)

JENNIFER ARIN is the author of *Ways We Hold* and *The Roots of Desire*. Her essays and poems have been published in both the U.S. and Europe. She has written poetry segments for television and radio, and did the French-to-English translations for the film *The Adventures of Tintin*'s web site. Awards include grants from the NEH and PEN Writer's Fund, a Poets & Writers' Writers-On-Site residency, and a 2015 Distinguished Faculty Award from San Francisco State University, where she teaches.

MICHAEL AUTREY is a poet and a critic. He lives in Chicago and serves as the Writing Specialist for the University of Chicago Laboratory High School. His reviews and criticism have appeared in *Booklist*, *Consequence Magazine*, *The Oregonian*, *Literary Matters*, *Prodigal*, *Chicago Review* and culturalsociety.org. He is working towards an MFA at the Bennington Writing Seminars. The Cultural Society published *Our Fear*, his first full-length book, in 2013.

PAUL CYRUS BRAY was born in Washington, DC in 1951, grew up in Maryland, Spain, and Panama, earned a BA Bard College, and a PhD from CUNY (dissertation on *Finnegans Wake*). Though he taught some, he was most proud of his work in the NY art scene in the 70s and 80s where he collaborated on films and sang his own lyrics for the band *Brains in Heaven*. He later lived in Santa Fe, where he died in 2011.

ANN CEFOLA is the author of *Free Ferry*, forthcoming in April 2017 from Upper Hand Press; *Face Painting in the Dark* (Dos Madres Press, 2014); *St. Agnes, Pink-Slipped* (Kattywompus Press, 2011); *Sugaring* (Dancing Girl Press, 2007); and the translation *Hence this cradle* (Seismicity Editions, 2007). A Witter Bynner Poetry Translation Residency recipient, she also received the Robert Penn Warren Award judged by John Ashbery. For more about Ann, see www.anncefola.com and www.annogram.blospot.com.

JON CURLEY is the author of the Dos Madres titles *New Shadows* (2009) and *Angles of Incidents* (2012). *Hybrid Moments* was published by Marsh Hawk Press in 2015. A Senior University Lecturer in the Humanities Department at New Jersey Institute of Technology, Curley has also written the critical volume *Poets and Partitions: Confronting Communal Identities in Northern Ireland* and co-edited (with fellow Dos Madres poet Burt Kimmelman) *The Poetry and Poetics of Michael Heller: A Nomad Memory*. He lives in New York City.

GRACE CURTIS's book, *The Shape of a Box*, was published in 2014 by Dos Madres Press. Her chapbook, *The Surly Bonds of Earth*, was selected by Stephen Dunn as the 2010 winner of the Lettre Sauvage chapbook contest, and she has been nominated for a Pushcart award. Her prose and poetry has been or is forthcoming in such journals as *Sou'wester, The Baltimore Review, Waccamaw Literary Journal, Blood Orange Review*, and others.

SARA DAILEY's *Earlier Lives* was a finalist for the 2012 Backwaters Prize in Poetry and her chapbook *The Science of Want* won the 2009 Shadow Poetry competition, while two of her poems have been turned into music by award winning composer Paul John Rudoi. Twice nominated for Pushcart Prizes, her writing has also appeared in *Creative Nonfiction, Asheville Poetry Review, New South, Cimarron Review*, and *Calyx*, among others, and on her blog at www.daileydiarist.com.

DENNIS DALY lives in Salem, Massachusetts with his wife Joanne. They have four adult children. Daly graduated from Boston College and has an MA in English Literature from Northeastern University. He has published three books of poetry: *The Custom House* (Ibbetson Street Press, 2012), *Sophocles' Ajax, a Modern Translation* (Wilderness House Press, 2012), and *Night Walking with Nathaniel- Poems of Salem*, (Dos Madres Press, 2014). Daly has worked as a dockworker, Union Leader of a 9000 member industrial local, and a city department head.

RICHARD DARABANER (1952-1985) left behind poetry, fiction, a dissertation draft on Kierkegaardian irony in Yeats and Rilke, and other prose. His poems have appeared in *Wanderings* and *Kateri*; his stories and the preface to his novel *Every Wound a Memory*, in the anthology *Phoenix Rising*; and his article on Thomas Pynchon, "A Possible Source for the Title of 'The Small Rain'," in *Pynchon Notes*. *Plaint*, a selection of his poems was edited by Daniel Gabriel, who also wrote the introduction. DANIEL GABRIEL has published three books: two book-length poems, or poetic works, on historical subjects, *Sacco and Vanzetti* (Gull Books, 1983) and *Columbus* (Gnosis Press, 1993), and a scholarly work, *Hart Crane and the Modernist Epic: Canon and Genre Formation in Crane, Pound, Eliot, and Williams* (Palgrave Macmillan, 2007).

DEBORAH DIEMONT lives in Syracuse, New York. Her poems from *Wanderer* and *Diverting Angels* have appeared in *Cairn, Stone Canoe, The Nervous Breakdown, The Raintown Review*, and other places. She spends summers traveling and working in Mexico and Central America with her husband and daughter.

JOSEPH DONAHUE's books of poetry include *Incidental Eclipse* (Talisman, 2003) and *The Copper Scroll* (Dos Madres Press, 2007), which is a section of an ongoing poem, "Terra Lucida." Three earlier sections have appeared as chapbooks. The most recent of these, *In This Paradise*, was published by Carolina Wren in 2004.

ANNIE FINCH is an American poet, author, and performer. She is the author of six books of poetry, most recently *Spells: New and Selected Poems* (Wesleyan University Press) and a dozen books about poetic craft, most recently *A Poet's Craft: A Comprehensive Guide to Making and Sharing Your Poetry* (University of Michigan Press). Annie collaborates frequently on musical, ritual, and theater performances and also writes nonfiction prose about spirituality for the *Huffington Post* and elsewhere.

NORMAN FINKELSTEIN is a poet, critic, and Professor of English at Xavier University. He has written extensively on modern poetry and Jewish American literature. His most recent critical book is *On Mount Vision: Forms of the Sacred In Contemporary American Poetry* (Iowa, 2010); his newest book of poetry is *The Ratio of Reason to Magic: New and Selected Poems* (Dos Madres, 2016). He is at work on a book of essays, tentatively titled *Like a Dark Rabbi: Modern Poetry & the Jewish Literary Imagination*.

347

KAREN GEORGE is author of the poetry collection *Swim Your Way Back* (Dos Madres Press, 2014), and four chapbooks, most recently *The Seed of Me* (Finishing Line Press, 2015), and *The Fire Circle* (Blue Lyra Press, 2016). Her work has appeared in *America, Adirondack Review, Naugatuck River Review, Louisville Review*, and *Still*. She reviews poetry at Poetry Matters: http://readwritepoetry.blogspot.com/, and is co-founder and fiction editor of the journal, *Waypoints*: http://www.waypointsmag.com/. Her website is: http://karenlgeorge.snack.ws/.

GERRY GRUBBS is an attorney who practices law in Cincinnati. He has had poems appear in numerous literary magazines and reviews. Dos Madres Press has just released his fourth collection with the press, *The Palace of Flowers*. His previous collection, *The Hive is a Book We Read for its Honey*, was a finalist for the Ohioana Library poetry book of the year, 2015. He conducts workshops under the names "Wordshop" and "Bringing More Creativity to Your Practice."

RICHARD HAGUE is author of fifteen collections of prose and poetry. *During The Recent Extinctions: New & Selected Poems 1984-2012* (Dos Madres Press) won the Weatherford Award in Poetry, and *Alive In Hard Country* (Bottom Dog Press) was the 2003 Appalachian Poetry Book of the Year). His second volume of collected poems, *Beasts, River, Drunk Men, Garden, Burst, & Light* is forthcoming in 2016 from Dos Madres Press. He is Writer-in-Residence at Thomas More College, Crestview Hills, Kentucky.

RUTH D. HANDEL's publications include one collection (*No Border Is Perennial*, 2015 Dos Madres Press), two chapbooks (*Tugboat Warrior*, Dos Madres Press, 2013; *Reading the White Spaces*, Finishing Line, 2009) and poems in anthologies and journals. A manuscript on work with psychiatric patients is in process. Ruth teaches poetry workshops, gives public readings, and leads the Poetry Caravan, an organization that brings poetry to hospitals and shelters. A retired college professor, she is widely published in the field of family literacy.

PAULETTA HANSEL was recently named Cincinnati's first Poet Laureate. Her poems and prose have been featured in journals including *Atlanta Review, Talisman*, and *Still: The Journal*, and on *The Writer's Almanac* and *American Life in Poetry*. She is author of five poetry collections including *Tangle* (Dos Madres Press, 2015.) Pauletta is managing editor of *Pine Mountain Sand & Gravel*, the literary publication of Southern Appalachian Writers Cooperative. She coordinated this anthology project.

MICHAEL HELLER has published over twenty volumes of poetry, essays, memoir and fiction, the latest being *Dianoia*. Recent books include *This Constellation Is A Name: Collected Poems 1965-2010*, *Beckmann Variations & other poems* and *Eschaton*. Among his many awards and honors are the Di Castagnola Prize, the NEH Poet/Scholar Award and the Fund for Poetry. A collection of essays on his work, *The Poetry and Poetics of Michael Heller: Nomad Memory*, was published in 2015.

MICHAEL HENSON is author of four books of fiction and four collections of poetry. *The Way the World Is: the Maggie Boylan Stories*, won the 2014 Brighthorse Prize in Short Fiction. His most recent work is a poetry collection, *The Dead Singing*, from Mongrel Empire Press. His poems, stories, essays, and journalism have appeared in many magazines and periodicals. He lives in Cincinnati with his wife Elissa Pogue.

R. NEMO HILL is the author, in collaboration with painter Jeanne Hedstrom, of an illustrated novel, *Pilgrim's Feather* (Quantuck Lane Press, 2002); a poem based upon a short story by H.P. Lovecraft, *The Strange Music of Erich Zann* (Hippocampus Press, 2004); a chapbook, *Prolegomena To An Essay On Satire* (Modern Metrics, 2006); and two collections of poems, *When Men Bow Down* (Dos Madres Press, 2012) and *In No Man's Ear* (Dos Madres, 2016). He is editor & publisher of Exot Books, www.exot.typepad.com/exotbooks

W. NICK HILL (Walter Nickerson Hill) born in Chicago, raised in São Paulo, Brazil; Emeritus professor of Spanish at Fairfield University, now lives in Port Townsend, Washington. Dos Madres Press published *And We'd Understand Crows Laughing* in 2012 and *Blue Nocturne* in 2016. Hill's poems have appeared recently in *Verse Daily*, *ArLiJo*, and *Más Tequila Review*. As a translator, he has numerous credits, such as *Biography of a Runaway Slave*, reissued in 2016 by Northwestern University Press. www.wnickhill.net

ERIC HOFFMAN is the author of several collections of poetry, including *The American Eye* (Dos Madres Press, 2011), *By the Hours: Selected Poems, Early & Uncollected* (Dos Madres Press, 2013), *Forms of Life* (Dos Madres Press, 2015) and *The Transparent Eye* (Spuyten Duyvil, 2016). He lives in Connecticut.

JAMES HOGAN grew up in western Oklahoma where his grandparents were homesteaders. He attended Oklahoma A&M, graduated from the University of Oklahoma and did his graduate study at Cornell. He taught Classics for thirty seven years and now lives in Meadville, Pennsylvania.

KEITH HOLYOAK was raised on a dairy farm in British Columbia, Canada. His work includes a volume of translations from classical Chinese poetry, *Facing the Moon: Poems of Li Bai and Du Fu* (Oyster River Press, 2007), as well as three volumes of original poetry published by Dos Madres Press. Keith is a Distinguished Professor of Psychology at the University of California, Los Angeles.

NANCY KASSELL's chapbook *Be(longing)* will be published by Dos Madres Press in 2016. An essay, "Almost Not," was recently published on the blog of the journal AGNI. The first English translation of the poem "Non omnis moriar" by Zuzanna Ginczanka (from the Polish, with Anita Safran) appeared on *AGNIOnline* and will be published in the Posen Foundation's 2017 volume of the *Library of Jewish Culture and Civilization*. Kassell lives in Brookline, Massachusetts.

DAVID M. KATZ is the author of two books of poems published by Dos Madres Press, *Stanzas on Oz* (2015) and *Claims of Home* (2011). *The Warrior in The Forest* was published by House of Keys Press in 1982. His poems have appeared in *Poetry, The Paris Review, The New Criterion, The New Republic, Notre Dame Review,* and *The Hopkins Review*. He lives in New York City and works as a financial journalist and editor.

SHERRY MOORE KEARNS, native of New York's Adirondack area, received her BA in English from SUNY Cortland where she coedited the literary magazine *Transition* with Burt Kimmelman. Kearns is the author of several chapbooks of poetry as well as essays on poetry and art. *Deep Kiss*, her first volume of poetry, released in 2013 and *The Magnificence of Ruin* (2015) were published by Dos Madres Press. She is currently at work on her third book of poetry, *The Solitary Elms*.

BURT KIMMELMAN has published sixteen books of poetry and criticism, some memoir, and some hundred articles on literature and art. Often anthologized, interviewed in print or online, he has been featured on National Public Radio. His ninth collection is *Abandoned Angel* (2016), following *Gradually the World: New and Selected Poems* (2013). He teaches at NJIT and lives in Maplewood, NJ with his wife, the writer Diane Simmons. More about him can be found at BurtKimmelman.com.

RALPH LA CHARITY, a known stranger, has followed the open poetry reading path across America's abundant Hide at least since the late '60s. His slim 2014 Dos Madres book of poetry and collage, *Farewellia a la Aralee*, was his first flat-spine volume of poetry to be published in twenty-nine years. Word has it that Dos Madres is preparing a second, and fatter, collection of his poetry and collage as we speak, due to appear shortly.

PAMELA L. LASKIN directs the Poetry Outreach Center at the City College of New York. Poetry collections include *Remembering Fireflies* and *Secrets of Sheets* (Plain View Press); *The Bonsai Curator* and *Van Gogh's Ear*; (Cervena Barva Press), *Daring Daughters/Defiant Dreams* (A Gathering of Tribes) and *The Plagiarist* (Dos Madres Press). Plain View Press recently published *It's All About Shoes*, her edited multi-ethnic anthology about women's relationship to shoes. *Ronit And Jamil, A Palestinian/Israeli Romeo and Juliet* in verse will be published by Harper Collins in 2017.

OWEN LEWIS's poetry has appeared in *The Mississippi Review, The Adirondack Review, Four Way Review, The Cumberland Review,* and *Mom Egg Review*, among others. 2016 honors include First Prize in the International Hippocrates Prize for Poetry and Medicine and Second Prize in the Kent and Sussex Competition. A physician and professor at Columbia University, he teaches with the narrative medicine group. He is the author of four collections of poetry: *March in San Miguel,* and from Dos Madres Press, *Sometimes Full of Daylight, Best Man* (winner of the 2016 New England Poetry Club's 2016 Jean Pedrick Chapbook Prize.) and *Marriage Map.*

RICHARD LUFTIG is a professor emeritus of educational psychology and special education at Miami University in Ohio who now resides in California. He is a recipient of the Cincinnati Post-Corbett Foundation Award for Literature. His poems have appeared in numerous literary journals in the United States and internationally in Europe, Asia and Australia.

AUSTIN MACRAE's poetry has appeared in numerous print and online journals, including *The Tampa Review, River Styx, The Cortland Review, Tar River Poetry, 32 Poems* and many others. He currently lives in Ithaca, NY, where he writes and plays music.

MARIO MARKUS, Professor of Physics in Germany and born 1944 in Santiago de Chile, has written 158 articles about self-organization in the natural sciences. He won an award from the Chilean Government for a CD-book with translations of Chilean poems into German. Markus' own poems have appeared in Spanish ("Punzadas") and in German ("Stiche"). He has written books on his computer art and on self-made ice-flowers. His aim is to unify art and science.
www.mariomarkus.com

PATRICIA MONAGHAN (1946–2012) had a lifelong interest in Mary as a young Catholic and as a leader in woman's spirituality. She was a Pushcart winning poet, a scholar of goddesses, and a social justice and environmental activist, publishing books of poetry, and scholarship. Ireland was the focus of many poems and a book on its spiritual geography. A Quaker, she co-founded the Black Earth Institute and the Association for Women and Mythology.

J. MORRIS has published fiction, poetry, and criticism in more than 90 magazines in the U.S. and Great Britain. *When I Snap My Fingers You Will Remember Everything*, a story collection from No Record Press, appeared in 2016. His work has been nominated for a Pushcart Prize and reprinted in *Twentieth Century Literary Criticism* and *Anatomy of a Short Story* (Continuum Press). *Staring Down the Sun*, his first novel, is forthcoming. He lives in Accokeek, MD.

RICK MULLIN's latest Collection, *Stignatz & the User of Vicenza* was published by Dos Madres Press in 2015. His other books published by Dos Madres are the booklength poem *Soutine* (2012), the collection *Coelacanth* (2013), and *Sonnets from the Voyage of the Beagle* (2014). His work has appeared in various journals and anthologies including *The New Criterion, American Arts Quarterly*, and *Rabbit Ears: TV Poems*.

FRED MURATORI is the author of three full-length poetry collections (*Despite Repeated Warnings, The Spectra, A Civilization*) and one chapbook *(The Possible)*. His poems, prose poems, and reviews have been appearing regularly in literary journals since the late 1970s. He lives in Ithaca, New York, and is the Bibliographer for English-language Literature & Film at the Cornell University Library.

ROBERT MURPHY's work has appeared in the literary periodicals *Smartish-Pace, The Colorado Review, Notre Dame Review, Cultural Society, Marsh Hawk Review, Beans and Rice, LVNG*, and the *Annals of Scholarship*. He is the author of a chapbook, *Not For You Alone* (2004), *Life In the Ordovician - Selected Poems* (2007), and *From Behind The Blind* (2013) - all published by Dos Madres Press. He is a 2000 winner of the William Bronk Foundation prize for poetry. Robert Murphy is executive editor and publisher of Dos Madres Press. He is married to the iconographer and painter ELIZABETH HUGHES MURPHY, who is both book designer and illustrator for Dos Madres Press.

PAM O'BRIEN has been writing poetry since she studied at Allegheny College. Over 100 of her poems have appeared in journals, magazines, newspapers and the small press. She has three chapbooks, *Kaleidoscopes, Paper Dancing* and *Acceptable Losses*. Her full-length collection, *The Answer to Each Is the Same*, was published by Dos Madres in 2012. Pam holds a lectureship at the University of Pittsburgh where she serves as Associate Director of Public and Professional Writing. She lives in Pittsburgh with her husband.

PETER O'LEARY has published several collections of poetry, most recently *The Sampo* (Cultural Society). He teaches at the School of the Art Institute of Chicago and, with John Tipton, edits Verge Books, an independent poetry press. He lives in Oak Park, Illinois.

BEA OPENGART's poems have appeared in numerous journals, and she has published three volumes of poetry: *In the Land* (Dos Madres Press, 2011), *This Day* (Finishing Line Press, 2011), and *Erotica* (Owl Creek Press, 1995). She has received grants from The Kentucky Arts Council, The Kentucky Foundation for Women, and The Ohio Arts Council. Bea teaches in the English Department at The University of Cincinnati.

DAVID A. PETREMAN was born in Kenosha, Wisconsin in 1948 and educated at Illinois Wesleyan University and the University of Iowa. He has published poetry in U.S. and Canadian literary journals as well as in Chile and France. He has translated into English and published the poetry of many Chilean poets. Poetry books include *Candelight in Quintero* (Dos Madres Press, 2011) and *Francisco in the Days of Exile* (Finishing Line Press, 2008.) He teaches Spanish Language and Latin American Literature at Wright State University.

PAUL PINES grew up in Brooklyn around the corner from Ebbets Field and passed the early 60s on the Lower East Side of New York. He has two novels *The Tin Angel* and *Redemption*. *My Brother's Madness*, a memoir, explores the unfolding of intertwined lives. He has published thirteen books of poetry including: *Fishing On The Pole Star, Message From The Memoirist* and *Charlotte Songs*. Pines is the editor of the Juan Gelman's selected poems, *Dark Times/ Filled with Light*.

DON SCHOFIELD's books include *In Lands Imagination Favors* (Dos Madres Press, 2014) *Before Kodachrome* (FutureCycle Press, 2012), *The Known: Selected Poems* [of Nikos Fokas], *1981 – 2000* (Ypsilon Press, 2010), *Kindled Terraces: American Poets in Greece* (Truman State University Press, 2004) and *Approximately Paradise*, (University Press of Florida, 2002). He is a recipient of the 2010 John D. Criticos Prize (UK), and the 2005 Allen Ginsberg Award (US), among others, and was a Stanley J. Seeger Writer-in-Residence at Princeton University. He has lived in Greece for many years.

DAVID SCHLOSS was born in Brooklyn, NY, and was educated at Columbia, USC Cinema School, Brooklyn College (BA), Iowa Writers Workshop (MFA). He taught at University of Cincinnati and Miami University (retired as Emeritus Professor of English, December, 2014). He's published four full poetry collections, three chapbooks and scores of poems in literary journals and anthologies over the years. He's also written occasional film reviews for AEQAI, an on-line arts magazine.

DANIEL SHAPIRO's most recent collections are *The Red Handkerchief and Other Poems* (2014) and *Woman at the Cusp of Twilight* (2016), both published by Dos Madres Press. He is also the translator of *Cipango*, by Tomás Harris (2010). Shapiro has received translation fellowships from the National Endowment for the Arts and PEN. He is a Distinguished Lecturer at The City College of New York, CUNY, where he serves as Editor of *Review: Literature and Arts of the Americas.*

MURRAY SHUGARS has published two poetry collections with Dos Madres Press, *Songs My Mother Never Taught Me* (2011) and *Snakebit Kudzu* (2012). He lives with his wife Sandra in Vicksburg, Mississippi, and teaches writing and literature at Alcorn State University.

JASON SHULMAN is an American spiritual teacher, poet and musician. He is the founder of A Society of Souls: The School for Nondual Healing and Awakening, based in the United States and the Netherlands. There he teaches the distinctive body of nondual work he has developed to awaken the human spirit. His paintings have been shown at the Provincetown Art Museum and the Hunterdon Museum of Art. He has published two books of poetry.

MAXINE SILVERMAN is the author of *Palimpsest* and four chapbooks: *Survival Song, Red Delicious (in Desire Path)*, inaugural volume of Quartet Series from Toadlily Press), *52 Ways of Looking, Transport of the Aim, a garland of poems on the lives of Emily Dickinson, Thomas Wentworth Higginson and Celia Thaxter.* Winner of a Pushcart Prize, she calls "Life List," inscribed on granite at Edmands Park in Newton, MA, her most unusual form of publication. She also creates collage and visual midrash (www.maxinegsilverman.com).

LIANNE SPIDEL is an Ohio poet from Detroit, member of the Greenville Poets. Her books are *What to Tell Joseme*, Main Street Rag Press, 2011, which won the Ohio Poet of the Year award, 2013, from the OPA; and *Bird in the Hand*, Dos Madres, 2014. Chapbooks are *Chrome*, Finishing Line Press, 2006; and *Pairings* (with artist ANN LOVELAND, member of Michigan Watercolor Society and National Watercolor Society), Dos Madres, 2012. Her poems have appeared in *Poetry, Shenandoah, Nimrod*, and other journals. She is mother of two sons and has five grandchildren.

OLIVIA STIFFLER worked for 26 years as a freelance stenotype reporter in Missouri. She began writing in earnest when she retired and moved to the South in 2006, where Dos Madres poet James Tolan discovered her in a writers' workshop. The two have been poet buddies ever since. Stiffler lives in Bluffton, South Carolina, among the alligators, egrets, and other wildlife, who, like herself, also appreciate the marsh grass, pluff mud, and pine trees that thrive near the Atlantic Ocean. She is hard at work on her second book.

CAROLE STONE is Distinguished Professor of English and creative writing, emerita, at Montclair State University. Her most recent poetry collections are *Late* (Turning Point, 2016,) *Hurt, The Shadow* (Dos Madres Press, 2013,) *American Rhapsody* (CavanKerry Press, 2012.) Her most recent poems have been published in *Slab, Exit 13, Cavewall, Bellevue Literary Review* and *Blue Fifth Review*. She received three Fellowships from The New Jersey State Council on the Arts. Carole Stone divides her time between Springs, East Hampton and Verona, New Jersey.

NATHAN SWARTZENDRUBER grew up in northern Indiana, a child of church musicians. He received BA and MA degrees in English, the latter from the University of Cincinnati. He currently lives in Cincinnati with his wife and two sons, where he is an ongoing contributor to Chase Public's Short Order Poetry project.

JEAN SYED was born in England and went to Birmingham University. Now she is in the Cincinnati Writers' Project. She has poems in *The Lyric, The Raintown Review, St. Anthony Messenger, Bird Watchers' Digest, For A Better World, Calamaro Magazine* and some which are defunct. Online she has poems in *The Road Not Taken* and *The Ghazal Page*. She has nature poems in her chapbook *My Portfolio* (Kelsay Books.) She has also been broadcast locally. Poetry is her hobby.

MADELINE TIGER's other published collections include *The Earth Which Is All* (2008) and *Birds of Sorrow and Joy: New and Selected Poems, 1970-2000* (2003). Her work appears regularly in journals and anthologies. She has been teaching in state programs and private workshops since 1973 and has been a "Dodge Poet" since 1986. She has five children and seven grandchildren and lives in Bloomfield, NJ under a weeping cherry tree.

JAMES TOLAN is author of *Mass of the Forgotten* (Autumn House Press), *Red Walls* (Dos Madres Press) and co-editor with Holly Messitt of *New America: Contemporary Literature for a Changing Society* (Autumn House Press). He lives in Brooklyn and teaches at the City University of New York. His website: www.jamestolan.com.

BRIAN VOLCK is a pediatrician who received his undergraduate degree in English Literature and his MD from Washington University in St. Louis and his MFA in creative writing from Seattle Pacific University. He is the author of a poetry collection, *Flesh Becomes Word*, and a memoir, *Attending Others: A Doctor's Education in Bodies and Words*. His essays, poetry, and reviews have appeared in *The Christian Century, DoubleTake, Health Affairs*, and *IMAGE*.

HENRY WEINFIELD has published three collections of poetry with Dos Madres: *The Tears of the Muses* (2005), *Without Mythologies: New and Selected Poems and Translations* (2008), and *A Wandering Aramaean: Passover Poems and Translations* (2012). His verse-translations include versions of the *Collected Poems of Stéphane Mallarmé* (University of California Press, 1995) and Hesiod's *Theogony and Works and Days* (with Catherine Schlegel, University of Michigan Press, 2006). He is a professor of Liberal Studies and English at the University of Notre Dame.

DONALD WELLMAN is a poet and translator. As editor of O.ARS, he produced a series of annual anthologies, including *Coherence* (1981) and *Translations: Experiments in Reading* (1984). His poetry is projectivist and works with sources from several languages. Collections include *Roman Exercises* (2015), *The Cranberry Island Series* (2013), *A North Atlantic Wall* (2010), *Prolog Pages* (2009). He has translated books by Antonio Gamoneda, Emilio Prados, Yvan Goll, and Roberto Echavarren. *Albiach / Celan: Reading Across Languages* is forthcoming (2016).

SARAH WHITE In the years since retiring from the French Department at Franklin and Marshall College, Sarah White has devoted herself to painting, poetry, and memoir. Dos Madres published *The Unknowing Muse* in 2014. It was succeeded in 2015 by *Wars Don't Happen Anymore* from Deerbrook Editions. The lyric memoir, *The Poem Has Reasons: a story of far love* is available on-line from Proem Press. She lives in New York City.

ANNE WHITEHOUSE is the author of six poetry collections—*The Surveyor's Hand, Blessings and Curses, Bear in Mind, One Sunday Morning, The Refrain,* and *Meteor Shower,* the latter two from Dos Madres Press. Her novel *Fall Love* was recently published in Spanish translation as *Amigos y amantes,* and her stories, features, reviews, and essays have been widely published in literary magazines, newspapers, blogs, and other publications. www.annewhitehouse.com

MARTIN WILLITTS JR. is a retired Librarian living in Syracuse, NY. He is the winner of awards including 2014 Dylan Thomas International Poetry Award; and *Rattle* Ekphrastic Challenge, June 2015, Editor's Choice. He has over 20 chapbooks, plus 11 full-length collections including *Secrets No One Wants To Talk About* (Dos Madres Press, 2011) and *How to Be Silent* (FutureCycle Press, 2016). His poems have appeared in *Blue Fifth Review, About Place, Kentucky Review, Perfume River Review, Bitter Oleander, Tipton Poetry Review, Nine Mile Magazine,* and others.

TYRONE WILLIAMS teaches literature and theory at Xavier University in Cincinnati, Ohio. He is the author of five books of poetry, *c.c.* (Krupskaya Books, 2002), *On Spec* (Omnidawn Publishing, 2008), *The Hero Project of the Century* (The Backwaters Press, 2009), *Adventures of Pi* (Dos

Madres Press, 2011) and *Howell* (Atelos Books, 2011). He is also the author of several chapbooks, including a prose eulogy, *Pink Tie* (Hooke Press, 2011). His website is at http://home.earthlink.net/~suspend/

KIP ZEGERS has been a high school teacher in New York City for 32 years. Much of his writing has grown from this work. His 9th and 10th books, both from Dos Madres, are *The Poet of Schools* and *The Pond in Room 318*. He lives with his family in The Bronx.

BOOKS BY DOS MADRES PRESS

◗ 2004

Annie Finch - *Home Birth*
Norman Finkelstein - *An Assembly*
Richard Hague - *Burst, Poems Quickly*
Robert Murphy - *Not For You Alone*
Tyrone Williams - *Futures, Elections*

◗ 2005

Gerry Grubbs - *Still Life*
James Hogan - *Rue St. Jacques*
Peter O'Leary - *A Mystical Theology of the Limbic Fissure*
David Schloss - *Behind the Eyes*
Henry Weinfield - *The Tears of the Muses*

◗ 2006

Paul Bray - *Things Past and Things to Come*
Michael Heller - *A Look at the Door with the Hinges Off*
Michael Heller - *Earth and Cave*
Richard Luftig - *Off The Map*
J. Morris - *The Musician, Approaching Sleep*

◗ 2007

Joseph Donahue - *The Copper Scroll*
Pauletta Hansel - *First Person*
Burt Kimmelman - *There Are Words*
Robert Murphy - *Life in the Ordovician*
William Schickel - *What A Woman*

◗ 2008

Michael Autrey - *From The Genre Of Silence*
Paul Bray - *Terrible Woods*
Eric Hoffman - *Life At Braintree*
Henry Weinfield - *Without Mythologies*

❯2009

Jon Curley - *New Shadows*

Deborah Diemont - *Wanderer*

Norman Finkelstein - *Scribe*

Nathan Swartzendruber - *Opaque Projectionist*

Jean Syed - *Sonnets*

❯2010

Gerry Grubbs - *Girls in Bright Dresses Dancing*

Michael Henson - *The Tao of Longing & The Body Geographic*

Keith Holyoak - *My Minotaur*

Madeline Tiger - *The Atheist's Prayer*

Donald Wellman - *A North Atlantic Wall*

❯2011

Pauletta Hansel - *What I Did There*

Eric Hoffman - *The American Eye*

David M. Katz - *Claims of Home*

Burt Kimmelman - *The Way We Live*

Bea Opengart - *In The Land*

David A. Petreman - *Candlelight in Quintero-bilingual ed.*

Paul Pines - *Reflections in a Smoking Mirror*

Murray Shugars - *Songs My Mother Never Taught Me*

Madeline Tiger - *From the Viewing Stand*

James Tolan - *Red Walls*

Martin Willitts Jr. - *Secrets No One Must Talk About*

Tyrone Williams - *Adventures of Pi*

❯2012

Jennifer Arin - *Ways We Hold*

Jon Curley - *Angles of Incidents*

Sara Dailey - *Earlier Lives*

Richard Darabaner - *Plaint*

Deborah Diemont - *Diverting Angels*

Richard Hague - *During The Recent Extinctions*

R. Nemo Hill - *When Men Bow Down*

W. Nick Hill - *And We'd Understand Crows Laughing*

Keith Holyoak - *Foreigner*

Pamela L. Laskin - *Plagiarist*

Austin MacRae - *The Organ Builder*

Rick Mullin - *Soutine*

Pam O'Brien - *The Answer To Each Is The Same*

Lianne Spidel & Ann Loveland - *Pairings*

Henry Weinfield - *A Wandering Aramaean*

Donald Wellman - *The Cranberry Island Series*

Anne Whitehouse - *The Refrain*

❰2013

Mary Margaret Alvarado - *Hey Folly*

John Anson - *Jose-Maria de Heredia's Les Trophées*

Gerry Grubbs - *The Hive-a book we read for its honey*

Ruth D. Handel - *Tugboat Warrior*

Eric Hoffman - *By the Hours*

Nancy Kassell - *Text(isles)*

Sherry Kearns - *Deep Kiss*

Owen Lewis - *Sometimes Full of Daylight*

Mario Markus - *Chemical Poems-One For Each Element*

Rick Mullin - *Coelacanth*

Robert Murphy - *From Behind The Blind*

Paul Pines - *New Orleans Variations & Paris Ouroboros*

Murray Shugars - *Snakebit Kudzu*

Jason Shulman - *What does reward bring you but to bind you to Heaven like a slave?*

Olivia Stiffler - *Otherwise, we are safe*

Carole Stone - *Hurt, the Shadow-the Josephine Hopper poems*

Brian Volck - *Flesh Becomes Word*

Kip Zegers - *The Poet of Schools*

❥2014

John Anson - *Time Pieces - poems & translations*
Ann Cefola - *Face Painting in the Dark*
Grace Curtis - *The Shape of a Box*
Dennis Daly - *Nightwalking with Nathaniel-Poems of Salem*
Karen George - *Swim Your Way Back*
Ralph La Charity - *Farewellia a la Aralee*
Patricia Monaghan - *Mary-A Life in Verse*
Rick Mullin - *Sonnets from the Voyage of the Beagle*
Fred Muratori - *A Civilization*
Paul Pines - *Fishing on the Pole Star*
Don Schofield - *In Lands Imagination Favors*
Daniel Shapiro - *The Red Handkerchief and Other Poems*
Maxine Silverman - *Palimpsest*
Lianne Spidel & Anne Loveland - *A Bird in the Hand*
Sarah White - *The Unknowing Muse*

❥2015

Stuart Bartow - *Einstein's Lawn*
Kevin Cutrer - *Lord's Own Anointed*
Richard Hague - *Where Drunk Men Go*
Ruth D. Handel - *No Border is Perennial*
Pauletta Hansel - *Tangle*
Eric Hoffman - *Forms of Life*
Roald Hoffmann - *Something That Belongs To You*
Keith Holyoak - *The Gospel According to Judas*
David M. Katz - *Stanzas on Oz*
Sherry Kearns - *The Magnificence of Ruin*
Marjorie Deiter Keyishian - *Ashes and All*
Jill Kelly Koren - *The Work of the Body*
Owen Lewis - *Best Man*
Paul Pines - *Message from the Memoirist*
Samantha Reiser - *Tomas Simon and Other Poems*

361

Quanita Roberson - *Soul Growing-Wisdom for thirteen year old boys from men around the world*

David Schloss - *Reports from Babylon and Beyond*

Eileen R. Tabios - *INVENT[ST]ORY Selected Catalog Poems and New 1996-2015*

Kip Zegers - *The Pond in Room 318*

❯2016

Anthology - *Realms of the Mothers-The First Decade of Dos Madres Press*

Eduardo Chirinos - *Still Life with Flies [naturaleza muerta con moscas]*, Bilingual, English translation by G. J. Racz

Norman Finkelstein - *The Ratio of Reason to Magic: New & Selected Poems*

Gerry Grubbs - *The Palace of Flowers*

Richard Hague - *Beasts, River, Drunk Men, Garden, Burst, & Light - Sequences & Long Poems*

R. Nemo Hill - *In No Man's Ear*

W. Nick Hill - *Blue Nocturne*

Nancy Kassell - *Be(longing)*

Rick Mullin - *Stignatz & the User of Vicenza*

Sharon Olinka - *Old Ballerina Club*

Bea Opengart - *Duties of the Heart, a Verse Memoir*

Michael Rothenberg - *Drawing the Shade*

Natalie Safir - *Eyewitness*

Daniel Shapiro - *Woman at the Cusp of Twilight*

Madeline Tiger - *In The Clearing*

John J. Trause - *Picture This: For Your Eyes and Ears*

Leonard Trawick - *A 24-Hour Cotillion*

John Tripoulas - *A Soul Inside Each Stone*

Panagiotis A. Tsonis - *An Autobiography*

Anne Whitehouse - *Meteor Shower*

Geoffrey Woolf - *Learn to Love Explosives*

David Almaleck Wolinsky - *The Crane is Flying - Early Poems*

Tyrone Williams - *Between Red & Green: Narrative of the Black Brigade*

www.dosmadres.com